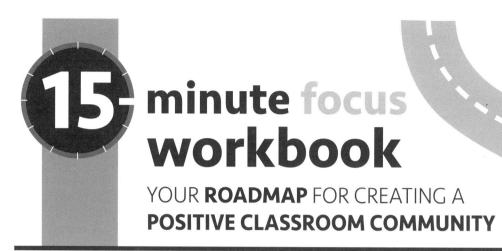

15-minute focus
workbook
YOUR **ROADMAP** FOR CREATING A
POSITIVE CLASSROOM COMMUNITY

BEHAVIOR
INTERVENTIONS

AMIE DEAN

NATIONAL CENTER for
YOUTH ISSUES

For every educator out there who pours your time, heart, and soul into your work — you are a gift to this world and all your efforts matter. Be proud of what you do.

I see you, and you amaze me!

– Amie

Funding to help underwrite the development of
the *15-Minute Focus* series has been generously provided by:

Maclellan Family Foundations

We partner with the courageous
to change the world.

The Sarah T. Butler Children's Center at the Pastoral Institute of Columbus, Georgia is dedicated to the mental health and well-being of children ages 1-18. This center provides comprehensive services that span psychological testing, intervention, therapy groups, and counseling. In all our activities we seek to inspire growth through faith, hope, and love.

Duplication and Copyright

NATIONAL CENTER for
YOUTH ISSUES
P.O. Box 22185
Chattanooga, TN 37422-2185
423.899.5714 • 866.318.6294
fax: 423.899.4547 • www.ncyi.org

ISBN: 9781953945716
© 2022 National Center for Youth Issues, Chattanooga, TN
All rights reserved.
Written by: Amie Dean
Published by National Center for Youth Issues
Printed in the U.S.A. • July 2022

Contents

**See page 210 for information about
Downloadable Resources and Templates.**

Introduction

After writing *Behavior Interventions: Strategies for Educators, Counselors, and Parents*, the feedback from teachers and administrators made it clear that educators are hungry for and highly interested in strategies and techniques to prevent student behavior challenges. They also shared that they feel very overwhelmed by the time it takes to find, create, or organize the tools to do it. *Behavior Interventions Workbook: Your Roadmap for Creating a Positive Classroom Community* was designed to simplify the process by finding, creating, and organizing the tools for you. Ask and you shall receive!

In twenty-first-century classrooms, teachers are expected to learn curriculum, teach the standards, learn and master the ever-changing technology, manage schedules, behavior, student work, and grades, and make connections, get to know students personally, and build positive relationships. And this is the short list, my friends.

To be able to accomplish so many goals with excellence takes an enormous amount of organization and planning. I designed this workbook to help with just that—organizing and planning your first weeks of the year to establish a positive classroom community while also providing tools to support and nurture your community all year long. This workbook is full of activities and solutions that will aid you in supporting your students in their development of life skills, peer relations, conflict resolution, and self-regulation skills. You will also find many behavior problem-solving ideas and tools to help you prevent and address challenges as they arise throughout the year.

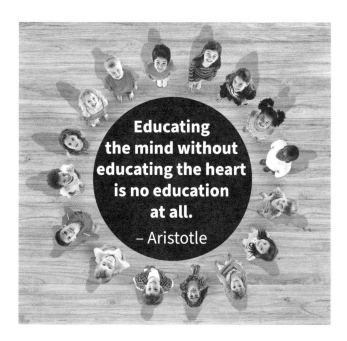

Educating the mind without educating the heart is no education at all.
– Aristotle

Purpose of this Book

Our main purpose as the adults who work in a school is to educate and care for the students who are entrusted to us. Many teachers have come to understand that we have to *connect* with students before we can *correct* students. As the familiar saying goes, for students to care how much we know, they have to know how much we care. This workbook will serve as your guide for how to set up and support a positive classroom community so you can get to the business of teaching content right away.

Before you dive into the how, I ask that you pause and consider your why. What drives you to spend most of your days with children or teenagers? What motivates you to do one of the most intense jobs on earth? I have identified certain principles that have guided my work with students who needed connection and caring more than anything else. I referred to it in Chapter 6 of *Behavior Interventions*, "Teaching with Heart— Five Principles for a Positive Classroom." I hope you will revisit these principles as you move through your year with the students who land in your room; each student is in *your* room for a reason. After reading these, please consider your why in your own words. On the difficult days and in the difficult moments, your why can be the fuel that keeps you going.

In a positive classroom community, educators believe:

1. Every child is born with unique gifts to offer the world.

2. There are no bad kids—just young people trying to cope and communicate the best they know how.

3. All behavior is an attempt to communicate a need.

4. Connection before content. Building community and connections will prevent many common concerns.

5. Our students' behavior is not our fault, but our response to it is our responsibility.

You may wonder why there is such a focus on building community and making connections in a workbook about behavior interventions? The answer is simple. *Building a sense of community and belonging in a classroom is the greatest prevention "strategy" a teacher can employ to avoid the most common behavior challenges.*

Of course, you will be teaching content and standards from the first week of school, but you can also include activities to help students feel *Connected*, *Capable*, and *Calm* in your setting. When we establish connections and a sense of belonging with and among our students, we create a sense of safety. When students feel safe or calm, they can take risks and are more open to learning new things.

Focusing on the 3 Cs in your first month will allow instructional minutes to be the focus of your daily practice for the remaining eight months.

After spending time building community by ensuring all students feel the 3 Cs, you may need ideas and tools for other aspects of a successful classroom. You will find tools for establishing rituals and routines to help your class run smoothly, applying management ideas for typical classroom disruptions, teaching mindset and goal setting, and implementing behavior support strategies for individuals or groups. The next section explains how these tools are organized so you can easily locate what best fits your needs.

How to Use this Book

The first step to a successful year is creating a classroom where students want to be.

In the *Journal of Educational Issues*, research about preparing students for adulthood notes, "Education, though constantly evolving, has one primary goal: to prepare students to be independent, responsible members of society. Though standards and curriculum change over time, one thing that remains constant is the necessity for life skills to aid students in their navigation through adulthood."[1]

Chapters 1 through 4 are full of activities for the first four to six weeks of school and are designed to create an environment where students feel the 3 Cs: Connected, Capable, and Calm right from the start. Many of the activities are also aligned with life skills that students will need to be successful in countless situations throughout their lives, not just as students in K–12 classrooms. The remaining Chapters, 5 through 8, are divided into specific collections of tools to meet specific classroom and student needs to sustain your positive community and address behavior challenges if needed. At the end of each chapter, you will find a planning guide, or chapter roadmap, to help you select the strategies or ideas that you want to implement. Many choices are offered, but I suggest only choosing the few that fit your needs as your year progresses.

Each year and each group of students is different. Your students will dictate what your community needs are; your final destinations and this roadmap will help you respond to those needs in a structured, deliberate way. My hope is that my thirty-year quest to find and develop activities that allowed me to successfully teach academics while also compassionately teaching humans helps you do the same.

NOTE: If you are in search of a comprehensive SEL program for school-wide implementation, an amazing resource is https://pg.casel.org/review-programs/, which has an extensive review of more than eighty options.

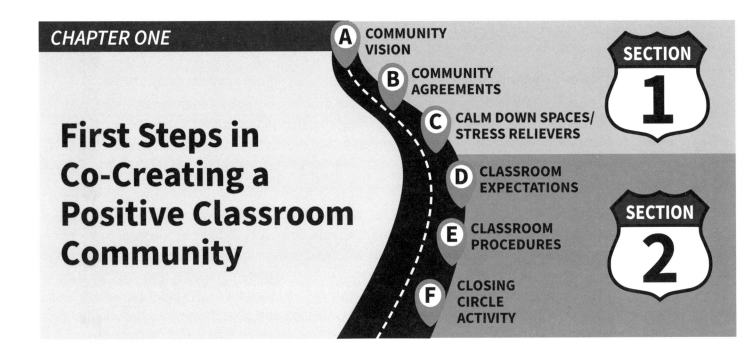

First Steps in Co-Creating a Positive Classroom Community

A — COMMUNITY VISION
B — COMMUNITY AGREEMENTS
C — CALM DOWN SPACES/ STRESS RELIEVERS
D — CLASSROOM EXPECTATIONS
E — CLASSROOM PROCEDURES
F — CLOSING CIRCLE ACTIVITY

SECTION 1

SECTION 2

If children feel safe, they can take risks, ask questions, make mistakes, learn to trust, share their feelings, and grow. – Alfie Kohn

Begin With the End in Mind

I have a few questions that I love to ask educators at the beginning of each new year. I bet you've heard similar prompts in your pre-planning faculty meetings or at a district-wide back-to-school event. I typically ask them to write their responses on sticky notes or respond to a poll so everyone can share their ideas.

What is the impact you hope to make on the students you teach this year?
What is the impact you hope to have on their lives?

If you had to condense your goals for your students this year into three sentences, what would they be? Would you say: *I want my students to grow and learn. I want my students to become responsible and independent thinkers or gain self-confidence in math. I want my students to feel loved.* Every teacher has hopes and dreams for the year—goals that get you going in the morning and push you to keep working hard for students even when you are past the point of exhaustion.

 Take a moment to think about three big goals or desired outcomes. If you utilize this book as your roadmap, these three goals can serve as your **3 Final Destinations**. Where do you hope to take your students this year and what do you want them to have when you get to the end?

1. _____

2. _____

3. _____

Knowing where you want your students to be in the end provides you with a mission. The 3 Final Destinations will help guide you in selecting activities from this book that will align with your students' needs, your teaching style, and the goals you hope to achieve.

At the end of this chapter, you will find a planning page: a checklist of the ideas from this chapter to help you choose and organize which activities will fit into your daily/weekly plans. The following pages are full of *options*—nobody can or should do all of them! Because schools are full of amazing people with different teaching styles, teacher personalities, and student needs, you will find a variety of activities from which to choose.

10 Student Skills for Success

The following skills are not meant to be taught in place of standards; they are necessary skills students must possess to learn and engage successfully with your content and standards. We all know that students need specific personal and interpersonal skills to help them navigate not only the classroom but also to find success in the workplace and in their personal relationships. Teaching the following skills identified in the five core competencies of CASEL—Collaborative for Academic, Social, and Emotional Learning—during the first month of school and throughout the year will help you create a learning environment where you are able to focus on teaching and learning instead of attending to behavior.

1. Respect for self and others
2. Recognizing strengths
3. Self-confidence
4. Identifying emotions
5. Stress management
6. Goal setting
7. Communication
8. Relationship building
9. Teamwork
10. Identifying and solving problems

Although there are more skills included in the CASEL 5, these ten are teaching priorities in the first weeks of school to establish the positive classroom community that we all strive to create. There will be many opportunities throughout the school year to teach these critical skills, not only during the first four weeks. They are embedded in multiple activities throughout this book to help promote and sustain your classroom community. Your students will benefit from your consistent coaching, including reminders and prompts, all year so new skills learned can become their daily practice.

NOTE: Unless you dedicate the time it takes to teach these skills early to prevent behavior issues, students will take your time later by presenting behavior issues.

First 2 Weeks: Establishing Expectations—the How To's

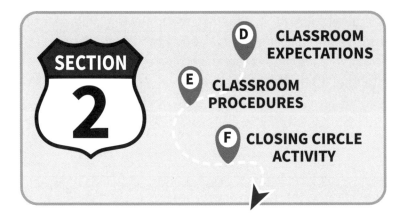

COMMUNITY VISION

Our Classroom Vision

Before establishing your Community Agreement, consider developing a Classroom Vision. A classroom vision includes the hopes and dreams of all students and teachers for the school year—the final destination. It allows all voices to be heard and for the teacher to get a sense of each student's personal goals.

You can solicit responses from students in one of several ways to allow them to share their vision for your class this year. After all students have submitted their hopes and dreams on any of the following templates, record the most common on chart paper, a bulletin board, or post in your online course as "Our Classroom Dreams Big," "From Vision to Victory!" or "#Hopes&Dreams for _____ (year)."

Options 1–3 for Elementary

Options 4–5 for Secondary

Big Dreams

Please write your name on the cloud.
Use the strips to share your big dreams for our classroom this year!

NAME HERE

BiG Dreams for ____ Grade!

Teacher Directions:

Give students a blank cloud template. Ask students to write 3 to 5 hopes and dreams for your class this year on colorful strips, and then they will glue them to their cloud.

On the cloud, students may write "I will" statements to establish personal commitments they will make to help their dreams come true.

OPTION 1: Big Dreams

This Year Is So Bright

Please write your name on the sun.
Use the sunbeams to share your hopes and dreams for our classroom this year.

Teacher Directions:

Give students a blank sun template. Ask students to write 3 to 5 hopes and dreams for your class this year on the sunburst strips. Students should cut out the strips and glue them to their sun. Post on your bulletin board or hang in a Hopes and Dreams Gallery.

Use the sunglasses to embellish your bulletin board, or print and write class goals on the sunglasses.

OPTION 2: This Year Is So Bright

The Sky is the Limit

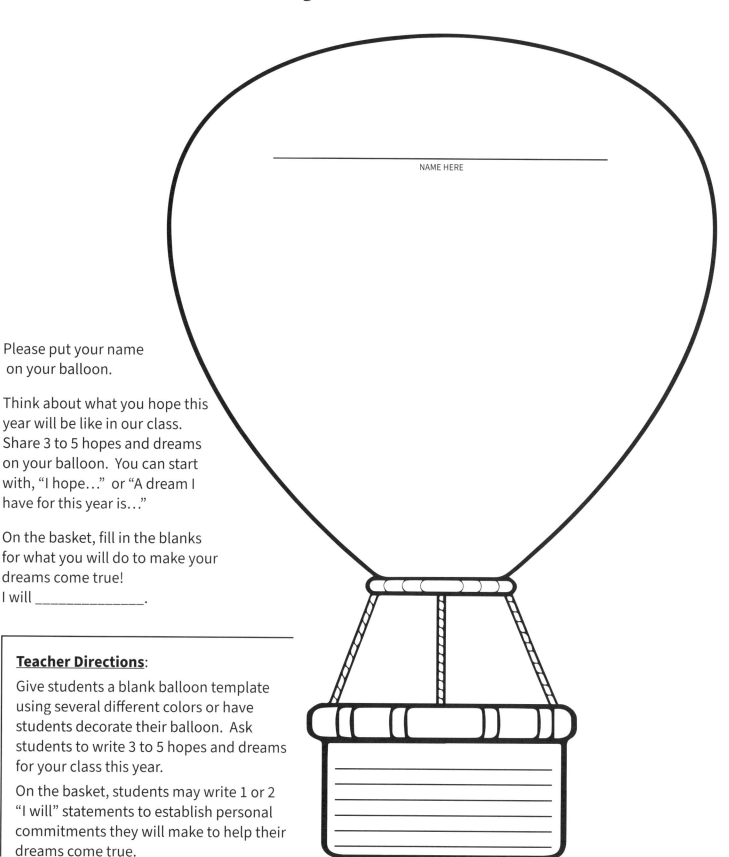

NAME HERE

Please put your name on your balloon.

Think about what you hope this year will be like in our class. Share 3 to 5 hopes and dreams on your balloon. You can start with, "I hope…" or "A dream I have for this year is…"

On the basket, fill in the blanks for what you will do to make your dreams come true!
I will _____.

Teacher Directions:

Give students a blank balloon template using several different colors or have students decorate their balloon. Ask students to write 3 to 5 hopes and dreams for your class this year.

On the basket, students may write 1 or 2 "I will" statements to establish personal commitments they will make to help their dreams come true.

Our Vision Board

Teacher Directions:

Pass out one copy of the #VisionBoard Activity Sheet to each student. Display their responses on a bulletin board or central location titled "#We'reTrending" or "#bestyearever."

#VisionBoard Activity
Please fill in each box with your response.

#Name:

#MyFaves

Artist or Band: _____

Song: _____

TV Series: _____

Restaurant: _____

Sweet Treat: _____

Thing to Do: _____

Place to Be: _____

#MyCrew
These people are important to me.

_____

_____

_____

_____

_____

_____

_____

#BigDreams

Write 3 personal hopes or dreams for your life.

_____

_____

_____

#SchoolGoals

Share 1 or 2 goals for this school year.

_____

_____

_____

#Let'sGo   If you could set up a field trip for our whole grade this year, where would we go?

_____

My Perspective

Think about your responses to the following questions.
Once you have answered them, write your answers on the cell phone template.

1. What do you hope to accomplish in this class?

2. Share 3 words you would use to describe the most successful class you've experienced.

3. Share 3 things you need from classmates to have a successful learning experience.

4. I hope my teacher will _____.

Teacher Directions:

Materials: My Perspective form for students, Chart Paper, Markers

• Pass out My Perspective form and ask students to respond individually.

• Once they are finished, form groups of 4-6 based on favorite type of candy (Skittles®, Sour Patch®, M&Ms®, Hot Tamales®, Reese's®, Starburst®).

• Ask them to select a recorder and highlight up to 3 responses for each question that represent their candy group.

• Each group will share, and the class will vote on top answers for each class to create your Classroom Vision Board.

1. _____
_____
_____

2. _____
_____
_____

3. _____
_____
_____

4. _____
_____
_____

Keys to a Successful Year

Bulletin Board, Poster, or Document in Online Classroom

• Allow students to write directly on the Classroom Vision Board or have them write on paper and staple to it so all students' ideas are represented somewhere in the responses.

• Use the Key Template (next page) to create a cohesive theme.

Statements to choose from:

A Successful Classroom Looks Like:

A Supportive Classmate is:

We Hope Our Teacher Will:

Room ___ 3 Keys to Success:

Teacher Directions:

Allow students to write their name and a response to one of the four statements on a Key Template. Use as many copies of the template as needed and then post in a central location as the "Keys to a Successful Year."

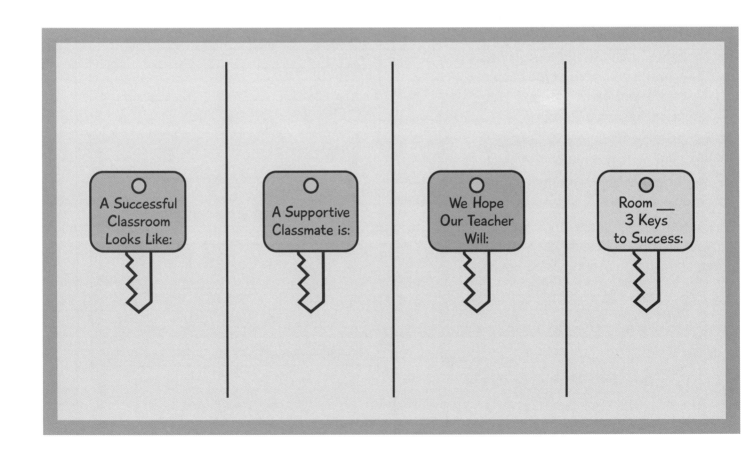

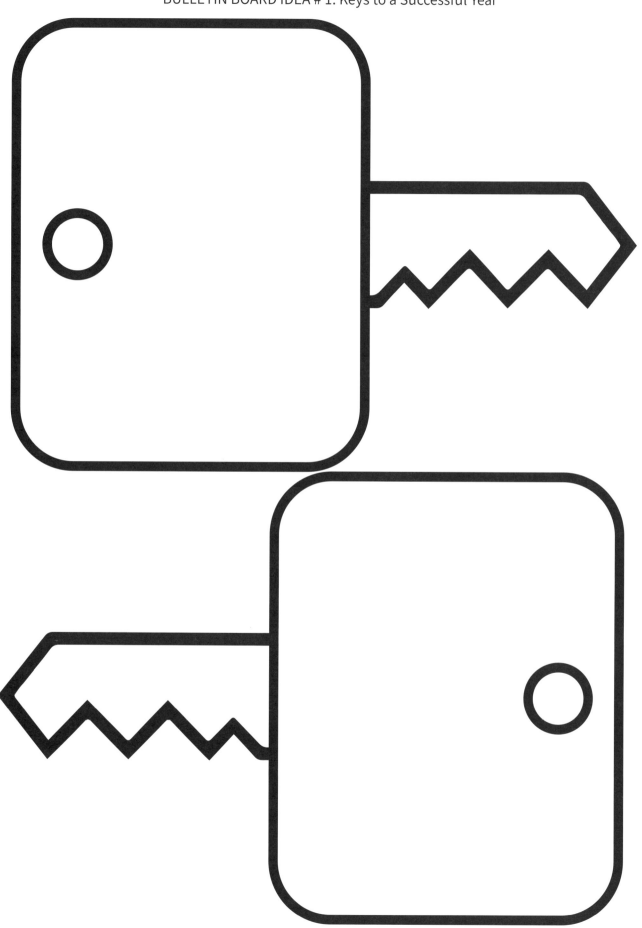

In This Class, We All FIT IN!

Teacher Directions:

- Assign or have students choose a puzzle piece below. Ask each student to write their name and one or two goals for the year on it then cut it out.
- Use as many copies of the template as needed.
- Encourage students to be creative and decorative.
- Post in a central location as one large puzzle.

COMMUNITY AGREEMENTS

This is a first-week activity as you are establishing how everyone will treat one another so everyone feels welcome, safe, and included. These three feelings are critical to maintaining a safe, positive learning environment. I suggest developing your Community Agreement *with* your students. If you teach multiple classes, all classes will have input, but only one final document will be posted.

Teacher Directions:

Using chart paper or bulletin board paper:

1. First, share your non-negotiables about respect. These are 2 to 3 things that are very important to *you*, the teacher, about how students will speak to you and one another. Be very clear and teach them what it *looks* and *sounds* like. Examples:

   • I will not yell, and students will not yell.

   • We will learn other ways to ask someone to leave us alone or stop talking.

   • "Shut up" is not allowed.

2. Next, teach coping skills or acceptable strategies to calm down. You may want to ask a few questions to introduce the idea of self-regulation. I refer to these ideas as Coping Strategies, Cool Downs, or Stress Relievers. There are also many videos on YouTube and books to read to younger students to introduce the concept of self-regulation. I typically have a 15–20 minute discussion with students beginning with these questions:

   • Have you ever felt angry at someone you love? (Teacher responds: Yes, me too.)

   • Have you ever felt so frustrated with something you couldn't do, you quit trying? (Yes, me too.)

   • Have you ever felt so sad about something, you thought you were never going to get over it? (Yes, me too.)

   It is okay for you to feel your feelings. It is not okay to disrupt teaching and learning.

   Explain that humans of all ages experience these feelings, and sometimes they are hard to manage. Ask students to share different ways they work through hard emotions or calm themselves down. If any of their strategies will work for your setting, include them in this section of the poster. You may also offer three to five alternatives to yelling, destroying property, walking out, etc., for your classroom.

   NOTE: The Calm Down Space will be explained, modeled, and practiced during weeks 1 and 2 for ALL grade levels and throughout the first month for elementary grade levels.

3. Finally, for part three, the teacher asks the students, "How do you want me to treat you? What does respect look and sound like to you?" The teacher can either write responses as students share, or have the students talk in small groups and respond on sticky notes. Once all responses have been shared on the board, group the similar responses, and choose four to five that represent the consensus.

   Examples:

   • We will use calm voices.

   • We will hold each other accountable respectfully.

   • We will be inclusive.

   • We will apologize when we mess up.

   • We will control our emotions or ask for help.

   • We are a team in this classroom.

Community Agreement
Room _____

Teacher Expectations (non-negotiables)

✓ _____

✓ _____

✓ _____

✓ _____

2. Classroom Calm Downs

✓ _____

✓ _____

✓ _____

✓ _____

3. Class Agreements—In Room _____ we will:

✓ _____

✓ _____

✓ _____

✓ _____

peace.

it does not mean to be in a place where there is no noise, trouble, or hard work. It means to be in the midst of those things and **still be calm in your heart.**

(unknown)

Calm Down Spaces

Self-regulation is an important skill students need in order to make learning happen.[2] Research has demonstrated that children who are able to better manage their thoughts, feelings, and actions are better able to succeed in social and learning environments.[3] Students who can manage their emotions effectively have also shown a foundation for positive classroom behavior and achievement.

Self-regulation, or being able to calm yourself when you are upset or feeling out of control, is a learned skill that must be modeled and taught. Just as children are taught to tie their shoes or ride a bike when they develop their fine motor skills, when a child's brain is developmentally ready to self-regulate, they can learn different strategies that work well for them. Consider what worked well for you the last time you felt angry, frustrated, anxious, or any other negative feeling. Did you go outside to get fresh air? Did you exercise? Take ten deep breaths? Go to your favorite place or call a trusted friend? We all have different coping skills and strategies we've learned to use to regulate our emotions and return to a more neutral or positive space. Our students are no different!

Many teachers in primary or elementary classrooms have implemented a calm down space to help students manage emotions, but it is not as prevalent in secondary classrooms. Every educator who has ever worked in a secondary classroom can tell you that older students also need support and guidance for finding calm when they are upset—the need does not magically disappear because a student has hit adolescence. If anything, the need for strategies, guidance, and support increases as the stress and pressures of school and life become more prevalent.

NOTE: I suggest introducing the calm down space while developing and finalizing the Community Agreement.

Helpful Hints:

✓ Pre-teach your expectations.

✓ Practice movement to the calm space, use of space, and how to return to their seat.

✓ Post your expectations in the calm space. Pictures/visuals for PreK–3.

✓ Provide reminders of those expectations often.

✓ Review what worked and didn't work when a student uses the intervention for self-regulation.

✓ Avoid using as a time-out/punitive space. Voluntary is best.

NOTE: I encourage you not to give up on offering this resource because students request it too often or spend too much time in it initially. These two issues typically work themselves out after 4 to 6 weeks as the novelty of the idea wanes, and the students who really need it will continue use.

The following variations of calm down spaces are intended for the PreK through 12th grade classrooms. Please consider which ONE will work best for your setting and start there. You will find that students may need multiple opportunities to "get it right" when requesting or using the space.

Calm Down Space Ideas for Elementary

Ideas for Names

- Calm Down Corner
- Think Spot
- Zen Zone
- Cozy Corner
- Safe Space
- Chill Chair

Google Images – Calm Down Spaces

https://www.littlemisskimsclass.com/2019/09/creating-peace-corner-or-calm-down.html

Pinterest – no author noted

Resources/Ideas/Images to Help You Set Up

- https://www.weareteachers.com/calm-down-corner/
- https://www.littlemisskimsclass.com/2019/09/creating-peace-corner-or-calm-down.html
- https://www.creativelyteachingfirst.com/blog/calm-down-corner-in-classroom
- https://www.boredteachers.com/post/20-inspiring-calm-down-corner-options-for-your-classroom

Books for Read-Alouds/Use in Calm Down Space

- *How To Crack Your Peanut* by Allison Edwards
- *I Am Peace* by Susan Verde
- *Your Happy Heart* by Amie Dean
- *Find Your Calm* by Gabby Garcia
- *I'm Stretched* by Julia Cook

Visuals To Use in Calm Down Space

The following pages can be used as the printed documents that will be posted in your calm down space. Choose what works best for you.

The area should include:

1. Calm Down Expectations
2. Calm Down Choices Poster
3. Feelings Chart
4. Reflection Form
5. Calm Down Kit (K–4) or Stress Relievers/Fidget Tools (5–12)
6. Include a place for the student to sit. The floor, a chair, or a desk works.

Calm Down Space Expectations

Use an Expectations Poster to post your expectations about how students should use their time wisely while in the Zen Zone. When introducing the area, review the expectations and follow up with several students modeling for the class the Do's and Don'ts of the area. This may take several repetitions before you see students using it appropriately without prompting or monitoring.

Ask the teacher for a break.

Set the timer for _____ minutes.

Choose ONE Calm Down strategy you will use.

Use the tools SAFELY and QUIETLY.

Clean up.

Walk quietly back to your seat.

CALM DOWN CHOICES

Deep Breaths

 **Write or Draw**

Squeeze an Object

 **Sit and Relax**

Use a Sensory Tool
(Play-Doh®, sensory bottle, or stretchy band)

 **Build with LEGOs®**

CALM DOWN CHOICES

 **Read**

Listen to Music

Push the Wall

 **Jumping Jacks**

Tear Up Towel

 **Think Happy Thoughts**

Feelings Chart

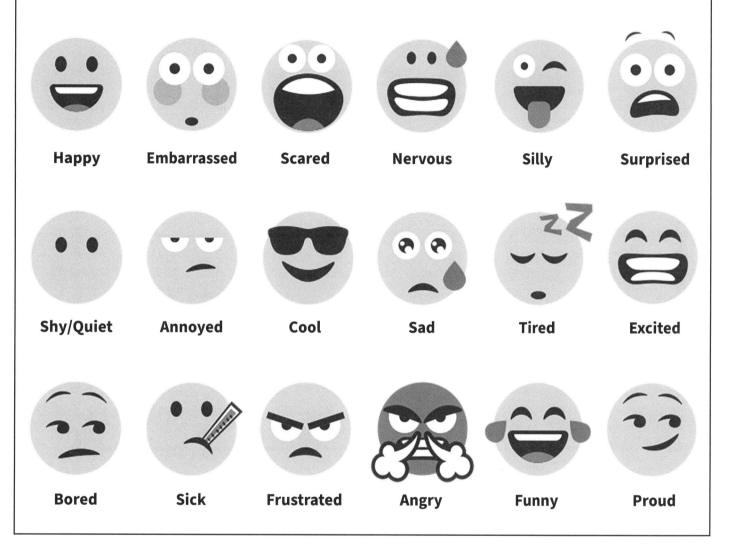

Happy	**Embarrassed**	**Scared**	**Nervous**	**Silly**	**Surprised**
Shy/Quiet	**Annoyed**	**Cool**	**Sad**	**Tired**	**Excited**
Bored	**Sick**	**Frustrated**	**Angry**	**Funny**	**Proud**

Teacher Directions:

Post the Feelings Chart in your designated space so students can use a visual to identify and name the emotion they are feeling. If the teacher interacts with the student while in the calm down area, ask them to share how they are feeling by using words or pointing to the image.

Calm Down Reflect and Return Form

Students can fill out a reflection form to show they are ready to return to their area or group.

Reflection

How are you feeling?

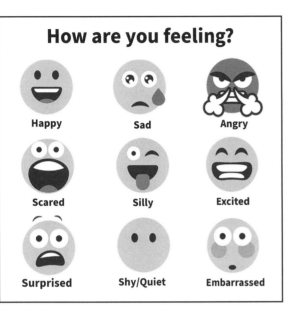

Happy Sad Angry

Scared Silly Excited

Surprised Shy/Quiet Embarrassed

What happened?

What can you do differently next time?

How do you feel now?

NOTE: I use the following language when discussing feelings with students:

✓ It's okay to feel _____, and I know how you feel. It can be hard to manage.

✓ Which calm down strategy worked for you?

✓ I am proud of you for handling this on your own.

We are more likely to see repetition of positive behavior choices if we pay attention to it and give it at least *equal energy* if not more energy than we give to negative behaviors.

Calm Down Space Ideas for Secondary

Ideas for Names

- Peace Corner
- Zen Zone
- Relax & Reboot
- De-escalation Space

In middle school and high school classrooms, we often see limited space due to class size and sheer mass of students. Placing a chair or one desk off to the side in a designated area may be all you can do with the space you have. Great! Do it. Please do not let lack of a large space deter you from creating this area for separation and self-regulation. For several years, I had a chair pulled over close to the wall with a piece of copy paper taped over it that said, "ALASKA." This is where you could go to cool off. Nothing fancy nor creative—just available.

Peace Corner

Teacher Directions:

The Peace Corner is a designated space for students to find peace within a few minutes and then attempt to positively rejoin the group. I suggest 3 to 5 minutes using a sand timer or digital timer with a very quiet beep to keep the avoidance behaviors at bay.

Helpful Hints:

✓ Find a spot for students to remove themselves from a stressor in your classroom. If it can have some barrier that allows you to still see them, good.

✓ Provide a place to sit and some scratch paper and writing supplies.

✓ Hang the Peace Corner Posters in the space.

✓ Provide a sand timer or small digital timer.

✓ You can include a few sensory items—stress relievers—if they fit your student needs.

(A teacher in Rockdale County, Georgia, who taught tenth graders had over twenty stuffed dragons that he called Emotional Support Dragons. I saw several students holding one while they worked on their computers, and he shared that his students use them every day!)

☮ PEACE CORNER

WRITE OR DRAW	**DEEP BREATHING**
YOUR CHOICE	**THINK OF YOUR HAPPY PLACE**

PEACE CORNER

COOL OFF IN THE PEACE CORNER

Using the Peace Corner

1. RETREAT: Walk away and calm down in the Peace Corner.

2. REFLECT: Think about what's upsetting you and how the issue might be solved.

3. RELATE: Ask for help or try to work out the issue if you're ready.

4. RETURN: Rejoin the group.

Reflect & Return

I am feeling _____ because _____

_____

_____

_____

When did this happen?_____

_____

_____

_____

I struggled with (circle all that apply)

Respect   Kindness   Cooperation   Compassion for Others

Personal Responsibility   Staying Calm   Listening to Others   Considering Perspectives

Next time, I will_____

_____

_____

_____

Something I can do to make today better is _____

_____

_____

_____

Stress Reliever Tools

The following ideas do not require a designated space in the classroom although they could be used in conjunction with the calm down space. These options allow students to use the strategy while in their own seat. You may list any of these as options in part two of your Community Agreement.

1. Frustration Card

The frustration card is a laminated colored square that allows students to "tap out" briefly. The teacher decides the set time and uses a sand timer or digital timer to regulate usage. The student is allowed to sit quietly at their designated seat and not participate while working through emotions and finding calm. See the Frustration Card template that you can print and cut out for student use.

Teacher Directions:

- Use colored index cards or pieces of laminated construction paper.
- Set the cards in a designated place in the classroom.
- When a student feels frustrated, they may get a card and place it on their desk. This indicates that they need a "tap out."

Helpful Hints:

Be sure to set parameters for the cards when you explain how to use this intervention.

✓ How long do they get to keep the card? (3–5 minutes)

✓ How often can they get a card? (Once a week/ three times per nine weeks—this varies depending on student age and teacher tolerance)

✓ Do they have to complete their work while they have the card? (If they only get to keep it 1–5 minutes, then that is up to you, but if they are allowed to keep it longer, I recommend that they still work, but they are not rushed.)

I'm taking a
quick break.

I'm taking a
quick break.

I'm taking a
quick break.

I'm taking a
quick break.

I'm taking a
quick break.

I'm taking a
quick break.

2. Fidget or Stress Box Calm Down Kit

Teacher Directions:

Collect fidgets, stress balls, or any other objects that can be used to prompt calming and focus, and place them in a designated area of the room.

When a student is stressed or fidgety, they may use an item from the bucket while they are in the Zen Zone or while they work.

Helpful Hints:

Be sure to set parameters for the fidget bucket when you explain how to use this intervention.

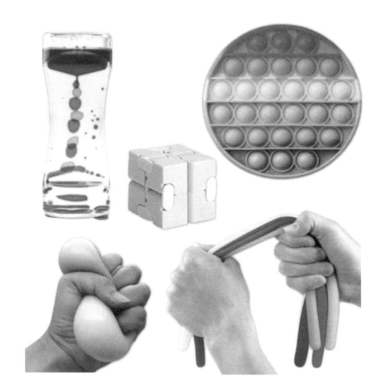

✓ How long do they get to keep the object?

✓ When do they get the object?

✓ How often can they have an object?

✓ What happens if they misuse the object or do not complete their work?

Use a basket or bucket filled with items such as stress balls, Play-Doh®, stretchy key rings, beaded necklaces, or sensory bottles, which are cheap and easy to make!

These DIY sensory bottles can be filled with vegetable oil or baby oil, food coloring, dish soap, glitter, beads, or crayon shavings.
BE SURE TO HOT GLUE AND TAPE THE LIDS!

3. Emoji Cubes!

I love these, and you can make your own with foam dice and paper or purchase them on Amazon. Search "Soft Foam Emoji Cubes."

Teacher Directions:

Students can use these while in the calm down area or at their desk as a squeeze object. These can also be used during class meetings to generate discussion around emotions and how to handle them.

Helpful Hints:

✓ Set a time limit for how long they should be used.

✓ If these are thrown or used inappropriately, they are removed as an option for one week.

✓ Remind students to use them in a way that does not disrupt others.

Check out https://www.weareteachers.com/fidget-toys/ for more ideas.

4. Listening Station

Teacher Directions:

Provide headphones and access to calming music via YouTube playlists, CDs, or a music subscription site with designated playlists for meditation or relaxation. You may want to play music for the whole class to listen to, especially in the morning, upon return to the classroom throughout the day, or during transitions. Some suggestions to search on YouTube are:

- Music 60 bpm (All grades)
- KidZen Music (PreK–2)
- Black Violin (All grades)
- Chillhop or Lofi (All grades)
- Piano Guys (All grades)
- Aquarium Music (PreK–5)
- OCB Relax Music
- Watch calming videos with headphones

5. Take the Temperature (K–12)

Examples:

5 – awesome, amazing, fabulous, epic

4 – great, lit, super

3 – good, average, fine, ok

2 – bad, unpleasant, frustrated (may need a check-in from adult)

1 – sad, terrible, awful (needs support from an adult)

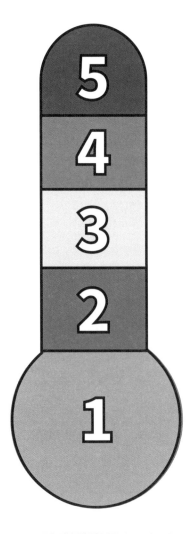

CLASSROOM EXPECTATIONS

People are often confused about the difference between "rules" and "agreements." In a classroom, our choice of words and approach can have a significant impact on student motivation and response. I am sure you have worked with a student who struggled with compliance and verbal commands; it makes for a long day and an even longer year. When we use language that is invitational versus directive, we are more likely to see students make positive choices.

Joshua Freedman, leader of Six Seconds' Emotional Intelligence Network, explains it like this: "Rules are for compliance."

Rules are imposed. They're set for the purpose of compliance. Mistakes should be punished to maintain power. Rules are "above people." When some students realize they don't have any power, they can feel pushed toward obedience rather than internal motivation.

Agreements are negotiated. They're set for the purpose of achieving common goals through collaboration. Mistakes should be discussed in order to learn from them. Agreements are between people in the group. The environment allows members of the group to have power so people are pushed toward <u>intrinsic motivation</u>.[4]

Teacher Directions:

You may choose to use the Community Agreement format for establishing your expectations or maybe you prefer to stick with a more traditional list of rules/expectations numbered and posted. Either way, please allow student discussion, healthy debate, and input in the final product. You will have much greater buy-in throughout the year when you can say, "This is what we decided on and agreed to do. I am upholding our agreements, and I am asking you to do the same."

Remember, choose only ONE of the following lists for your classroom expectations or make up your own. Once the final product is decided, post in multiple places in your space and refer to it often.

OPTIONAL LISTS OF EXPECTATIONS

Option 1: Our Classroom Expectations (3–12)

- Feel free to do anything that does not cause a problem for anyone else.
- I teach when there are no distractions or other problems.
- I listen to students who raise their hand.
- I listen to one person at a time.
- Please treat me with the same respect I treat you.
- If someone causes a problem, I will do something.

From Teaching with Love and Logic
(https://www.loveandlogic.com/pages/how-to-create-a-love-and-logic-classroom)

Option 2: Our Ready Position (PreK–2)

This list includes minimal words and works well for our youngest learners. They will need many repetitions of seeing, hearing, saying, and practicing these expectations as many are just learning how to work in a group away from their families with so many rules and expectations. The adjustment phase can sometimes be intense. Please note that it will take some students four to six weeks before you start to see unprompted practices, while others can take three to four months. Please don't be discouraged– keep coaching!

Option 3: Our 5 Rules (K–4)

Modified from www.wholebrainteaching.com, these rules are taught using hand gestures to help students remember the class expectations. I have modified Rule #5 to make it more about the community than the teacher. You can watch a video of an expert teacher teach the gestures here: https://tinyurl.com/ydzb4byk

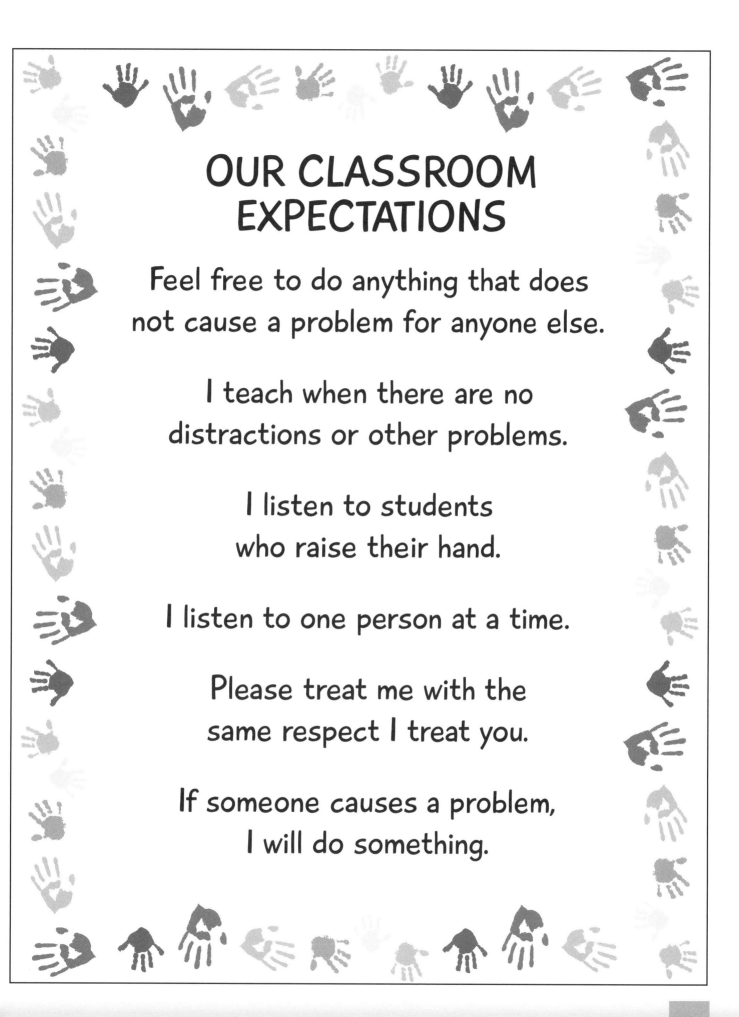

OUR CLASSROOM EXPECTATIONS

Feel free to do anything that does not cause a problem for anyone else.

I teach when there are no distractions or other problems.

I listen to students who raise their hand.

I listen to one person at a time.

Please treat me with the same respect I treat you.

If someone causes a problem, I will do something.

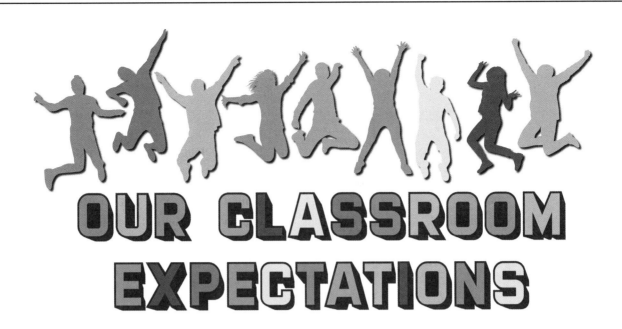

OUR CLASSROOM EXPECTATIONS

Feel free to do anything that does not cause a problem for anyone else.

I teach when there are no distractions or other problems.

I listen to students who raise their hand.

I listen to one person at a time.

Please treat me with the same respect I treat you.

If someone causes a problem, I will do something.

Our Ready Position

Rule #1

Follow directions quickly.

Rule #2

Raise your hand for permission to speak.

Rule #3

Raise your hand for permission to leave your seat.

Rule #4

Make smart choices.

Rule #5

Make our community better.

Designed using resources from Flaticon.com

OUR 5 RULES

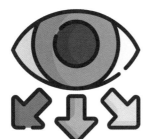 Looking Eyes

Helping Hands

 Listening Ears

Quiet Mouth

 Walking Feet

Designed using resources from Flaticon.com

CLASSROOM PROCEDURES

When routines and procedures are explicitly taught, modeled, and followed in your classroom, students know what's expected of them and how to do certain things on their own. Having these predictable patterns in place allows teachers to focus on meaningful instruction. The time spent teaching, modeling, and practicing procedures during the first weeks of school should not be viewed as a loss of instructional time. This time spent up front will help you avoid the frustration that repeated correcting and reteaching causes later in the year.

> *Student achievement at the end of the year is directly related to the degree to which a teacher establishes good control of the classroom procedures in the very first week of the school year.*
>
> **Harry Wong**
> *The First Days of School: How To Be An Effective Teacher*

Teacher Directions:

To introduce procedures, explain the difference between procedures and expectations. Expectations or agreements are how we will treat each other with respect and keep everyone safe in the classroom. Procedures are how we will get things done in an efficient, organized way so we can get to the business of learning.

Teach and model a few procedures per day for the first week of school, and then continue modeling and practicing for four to six weeks as needed. If you typically start class with a warmup activity, use that time in the first four weeks to teach and practice procedures.

When we teach procedures, it is not enough to only tell students what to do; we must also show them how to do it. A great approach to follow is the *5 Steps to Teach Anything*.

Tell – tell students how you want them to do the procedure.

Show – model exactly how you want it done.

Practice – have students PRACTICE doing the procedure.

Feedback – share their number of stars out of 10. "That was an 8 out of 10—great job! Here's what you need to do to get to 10."

Review – ask several students to quickly state the steps of the procedure.

For many years, I had a binder with twenty-one single pages—one procedure per page that I referred to as our Procedure Manual (see Chapter 3 for specific procedures). Being able to follow the routines of an organization is an important life skill, so I always introduced it to my students while referencing employee manuals of businesses they know well.

Teacher Directions:

Explain to your students that when we go to work, there will always be policies and procedures that employees are expected to follow. Since we are Professionals in Training, we have our own manual for this classroom, and we will learn about and practice our procedures until we know them well.

Happy First Week!

Morning Procedure

1. Please enter the classroom quietly.

2. Unpack your backpack at your desk.

3. Hang up your backpack/coat.

4. Lunch magnet.

5. Turn in papers/notes for me.

6. Sharpen two pencils.

7. Fill out agenda, leave it on the desk.

8. Answer Morning Message question.

9. Read when finished.

10. When the timer goes off please be on the floor for Morning Meeting.

CLOSING CIRCLE ACTIVITY

Teacher Directions:

Share the Week One Reflection form with students prior to the end of the day on the last day of week one. Allow them some time to fill in the blanks and invite them to elaborate if they want to add more. Share with the students that you will be asking for their input throughout the year so their voices can be heard, and so you can use the information to make changes and improvements when needed. This is a community, and everyone's voice matters. At the end of the day, ask the students to circle up. Go around the circle and allow each student to share their response to each of the questions.

Helpful Hints:

✓ If you'd rather students stay seated for this activity, that works too.

✓ The purpose of any closing activity is to take the temperature of how students are feeling.

✓ With so many new ideas and expectations being taught throughout week one of a new grade and with a new group of people, it is important to check in and let them share their joys, hopes, or concerns.

Week One Reflection

Directions: Please fill in the blank of each statement. We will share in our closing activity on Friday. I welcome your feedback on our class!

Something new I learned this week was _____.

Something I am looking forward to this year is _____.

I hope we can _____ **in this class in the future.**

First Steps in Co-Creating a Positive Classroom Community
Chapter 1 Roadmap (Planning Guide)

Activity Choose 1 from each section	Action Items: What do you need to complete?	Date: When do you plan to use?	Page #
COMMUNITY VISION (choose one)			
Big Dreams (K-5)			
This Year Is So Bright! (K–5)			
The Sky Is the Limit! (K–5)			
#VisionBoard Activity (6–12)			
My Perspective (6–12)			
Classroom Vision Final Product: Key			
Classroom Vision Final Product: Puzzle			
COMMUNITY AGREEMENTS			
CALM DOWN SPACES/STRESS RELIEVERS			
CLASSROOM EXPECTATIONS (choose one)			
Class Expectations (3–12)			
Our Ready Position (PreK–2)			
Our 5 Rules (K–4)			
adapted from www.wholebrainteaching.com			
CLASSROOM PROCEDURES			
Morning Procedure			
CLOSING CIRCLE ACTIVITY			
Week One Reflection Form			

CHAPTER TWO

Building Connections and Confidence

A GETTING TO KNOW YOUR COMMUNITY

B CELEBRATE STUDENTS' GIFTS

C AIM FOR AWESOME

Connection before content. – Peter Block

Author, storyteller, and researcher Brené Brown defines connection as "the energy that exists between people when they feel seen, heard, and valued; when they can give and receive without judgment; and when they derive sustenance and strength from the relationship."[5]

The first few weeks include dedicated time for building a sense of belonging where students feel welcome, safe, and included. Students having a sense of belonging where their voice and identity matters is an intrinsic motivator that will help them focus and work through hard times when learning or relationships become challenging.

As we get into week two, you will find activities that allow the teacher to share more about themselves and find personal connections with students by identifying common experiences. You will also find activities that focus on recognizing the gifts and areas of expertise represented in your classroom. The gifts gallery or expert board are simple yet powerful tools in recognizing the individual talents and special qualities every student brings to your community. *Everybody* wants to belong and feel important. Taking time to ensure your students feel connected and capable is a powerful prevention strategy that will serve as a foundation for behavior support when the need arises.

GETTING TO KNOW YOUR COMMUNITY

Teachers always have so many things to introduce and explain in the first week that we don't always have the time to share a lot about ourselves! Sprinkle in a few opportunities in week two for your students to get to know you better.

Share Your Favorites! Share photos, history, and favorite things. Add details about how you developed your passion or obstacles you have overcome. Create a slide deck, a collage, or a one-pager about yourself because students love to know as much about you as they can.

Two Lies and a Truth: Create slides or a Kahoot that include two lies and one truth about you and allow students to guess which is true. Go back through and reveal the answers and let them know who was the most accurate in figuring out who you are!

10 in 10: My students always loved that I allowed "10 Appropriate Questions in 10 Minutes." They could ask anything they wanted as long as it was rated PG, school appropriate, and within the ten-minute time limit, and I promised to answer. It was funny to watch them struggle to come up with questions when they were given so much freedom. I've had some classes ask to do it more than once, so I provided several opportunities for them to ask more questions.

Check out a free "Intro the Teacher" slide deck here https://www.weareteachers.com/editable-meet-the-teacher-slideshow/

10 Ideas to Check & Connect in 5 Minutes or Less

One of the challenges we face once the first weeks have passed is finding time to continue the connection and team-building activities. We are typically full steam ahead with content, assessments, and grades. As a joke, I once asked a group of teachers if they would want to continue to date someone who only showed interest in them as a person the first week, and then never showed interest again. Can you guess the answer? NO! Most of our time during the school year will be dedicated to academics, as it should be, but if we don't continue to connect with students, we may see a loss in their efforts and interest in our content. Pick something from the following choices and use it once or twice a week or whenever you can fit it in:

1. **Stand at the Door** and ask students to say their name as they enter, and you repeat it to learn names.

2. **Question of the Day** – Ask every student the same question as they enter your room once or twice per week to make a personal connection. Check out: https://kidsnclicks.com/questions-of-the-day-for-kids/ for lists of questions.

3. **Guess the Number** – Hold a picture or jar with a lot of items. Ask each student to guess how many and let them know at the beginning of class who was the closest.

4. **Pick Your Greeting** – Handshake, high five, or fist bump at the door.

5. **Are You Ready?** – Ask students to share one thing they are ready to do when they enter.

6. **Roll and Tell** – Roll the die and use the poster to ask a specific question.

   a. **(Roll I):** What is your favorite food?

   b. **(Roll II):** If you could have a superpower, what would you choose?

   c. **(Roll III):** What is something you do really well?

   d. **(Roll IV):** What made you smile today?

   e. **(Roll V):** Who is someone you look up to?

   f. **(Roll VI):** Who is your favorite team?

7. **Where Would You Go?** – Ask each student at the door to tell you what country, restaurant, or outdoor venue they would visit if they could go anywhere.

8. **Rock, Paper, Scissors** – Play RPS with students as they enter!

9. **Favorites** – Ask students to share their favorite _____. (Song, artist, game, candy, etc.)

10. **Whiteboard Wisdom** – Hang a small whiteboard outside your door. Post a Word or Quote of the Day and ask students to use the word in a sentence or share their response to the quote.

Please choose what works best for you! It is not necessary to do these every day or with every single student. Just making the effort when you can as often as you can shows your interest in who your students are outside of your classroom content. Focusing on connection before content goes a long way!

Roll and Tell

Let's get to know each other!
Roll the die and share something about yourself.

 *What is your favorite food?*

 *If you could have a superpower, what would you choose?*

 *What is something you do really well?*

 *What made you smile today?*

 *Who is someone you look up to?*

 *Who is your favorite team?*

The two most important days in your life are the day you are born and the day you find out why. – Mark Twain

Why do we need students to feel confident to have a successful classroom community? Confidence is directly related to motivation, which drives us to push through difficult things and try again after failing. The more confident we feel when we see a new task or activity, the more likely we are to give it our best effort! Self-confidence also enables students to handle setbacks with ease rather than shutting down and saying, "I can't do this." Instead of being defeated by failure, confident students get up quickly, learn from their mistakes, and try again.

By allowing all students to recognize something at which they excel and share it with the group, we help them build confidence and a sense of contribution to the classroom. Students may identify attributes such as talking (yes, talking!), being kind, being helpful, or even being timely, in addition to sports, music, hobbies, and specific subject areas that students tend to cite as personal gifts. Once students have identified their areas of expertise, the following activities include ideas to highlight and celebrate every student in your classroom community. Choose what works for you.

Create a "Meet the Experts" Bulletin Board

Teacher Directions:

- Each student can either write their name and area of expertise directly on the bulletin board paper or hang the #MeetTheExpert Cards that can be grouped and changed out as needed.

- For grades K–3: ask students to complete the card and draw a picture.

- For grades 4–12: students can complete the card and add *how* they gained the knowledge that made them an expert.

- We want students to see a correlation between the amount of time and effort put into practice with a subject or activity and the level of confidence they feel in referring to themselves as experts in that subject or activity.

- Examples of *how* may include years of practice or involvement, reading about it, watching videos, listening to a family member, or other ideas.

Quotes for the "Meet the Experts" Bulletin Board:

Practice creates confidence. Confidence empowers you. – Simone Biles, Olympic Gymnast

The expert in anything was once a beginner. – Helen Hayes, EGOT Recipient

Practice makes perfect. After a long time of practicing, our work will become natural, skillful, swift, and steady. – Bruce Lee, Master of Martial Arts and Actor

I have standards I don't plan on lowering for anybody—including myself. – Zendaya, Actor, Singer, Producer

Practice isn't the thing you do once you're good. Practice is the thing you do that makes you good. – Malcolm Gladwell, Author and Speaker

Practice creates confidence.
Confidence empowers you.

Simone Biles

Olympic Gymnast

The expert in anything
was once a beginner.

Helen Hayes

EGOT Recipient

Practice makes perfect.
After a long time of practicing,
our work will become natural,
skillful, swift, and steady.

Bruce Lee

Master of Martial Arts and Actor

> *I have standards
> I don't plan on lowering
> for anybody
> —including myself.*

Zendaya

Actor, Singer, Producer

> *Practice isn't the thing
> you do once you're good.
> Practice is the thing you do
> that makes you good.*

Malcolm Gladwell

Author and Speaker

Meet the Expert Student Card

Teacher Directions:

- Introduce the word *expert* and ask students what it means.
- Ask them to talk about what it takes to become an expert.
- Ask them to brainstorm a list of things they have spent a lot of time doing.

Meet the Expert Presentations

Allow students to create a slideshow, poster, video, or other presentation and spend five minutes teaching or sharing their area of expertise to the class. You can choose one student to share once per week or several students per week as a closing activity for the day until all students have presented. Visit www.geniushour.com or https://tinyurl.com/y7oh6ceu for endless ideas and templates. This is a great confidence builder and community builder, and allows for various success skills like listening, communication, and respect for others to be taught in practice instead of isolation.

NOTE: Refer to students as the "Soccer Expert," "Reptile Expert," or "SnapChat Expert" when possible. It builds confidence in the individual and also highlights their special qualities so classmates see them for more than their daily behavior.

Gifts Gallery

A student Gifts Gallery is an opportunity for students to brainstorm the qualities about themselves that make them proud or unique, or highlight their contributions to their community or family. You can use the easy fill-in-the-blank poem that any student can complete after brainstorming their gifts.

Teacher Directions:

- Distribute the *What are My Gifts?* handout.
- Ask students to brainstorm as many personal gifts as they can think of in a certain number of minutes. They may need you to share ideas, such as playing football, cooking, styling hair, reading, playing piano, being a good listener, or being a good brother. If they can think of more than five, that is great and should be encouraged.
- Once they have their list, they should choose the three they want to share in the Gifts Gallery.
- Find a space in the classroom to hang twine or yarn. Use clips to display each student's Gifts Poem.

NOTE: If you want to get fancy, you can find lighted clips on a wire on Amazon to hang student pictures/products.

#MeetTheExpert

Name_____

I know a lot about_____.

Ask me a question about _____.

Draw here.

#MeetTheExpert

Name_____

I am an expert on _____

_____.

Gifts Gallery

What are My Gifts?

 Every person is born with special gifts, and we all have different gifts.

List 5 of your gifts: things you do well, know a lot about, or can offer to others.

STUDENT PHOTO HERE

1 _____

2 _____

3 _____

4 _____

5 _____

Fill in the poem with **3** of your gifts:

I'm _____

& _____ .

I'm _____, too.

I'll be me, and You be you.

Personal Bio Bag Project

This twist on the All About Me bag allows students to share external attributes that a person might know by looking at them on the outside of the bag. Inside, they should include items that represent things you might not know about them unless you get to know them personally.

Teacher Directions:

- Distribute paper bags and Bio Bag instructions.
- Show a model of your own bag completed.
- Explain that students should share 3 to 5 personal facts that others can *see* about them on the outside.
- Explain that they can add up to 5 items inside the bag that represent who they are. These are things others might not know unless they get to know them.

**I have also included a template of a person for grades K–2 to decorate instead of writing on the bag.

Personal Bio Bag Project

Your assignment is to create a bag that represents you—what the world sees on the outside and the real you.

- On the outside of the bag write or illustrate 3 to 5 identifiers that people may see when they look at you (hair color, height, ethnicity, style of dress, etc.).

- Next, find 4 to 5 items at home that represent you.

- All of your items must fit in this bag.

- Bring the bag back to school by _____ and be prepared to use the contents of your bag to tell about yourself.

- You may include anything you want, as long as it is appropriate for school. This means no living creatures, no weapons, and nothing that will spoil!

  Some possibilities include:
  - ✓ Photos of family and friends
  - ✓ Items that represent your favorite hobbies or activities
  - ✓ Favorite book
  - ✓ Special keepsake

All About Me

Directions: Draw picture of things we can see about you on your cutout. You can put eye color, favorite clothes and shoes, hair color, and jewelry. Have fun!

Learning Strengths Inventory and Activities

The idea of different learning styles and the often-debated Theory of Multiple Intelligences have been used in education for many years. Both suggest that humans have multiple ways of accessing and demonstrating new learning.

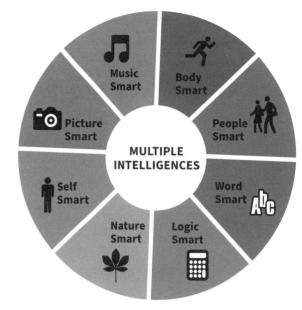

"Research shows that students are more engaged and learn best when they are given various ways to demonstrate their knowledge and skills, which also helps teachers more accurately assess student learning."[6]

In week three, the following activities are intended to support the positive classroom community in three ways: build student confidence, continue to highlight many areas of student strengths, and create a variety of ways student can demonstrate learning. We are not teaching students they possess isolated or limited areas of ability, but rather they have *many* areas of ability and all of them can be developed and improved with time, attention, and practice.

I love to share the following quote by Howard Gardner, the author of *Multiple Intelligences*: "It's not how smart you are, it's how are you smart?" Assure your students we are *all smart* in multiple ways. These activities allow you and your students to recognize and celebrate the many ways we are smart and capable as human beings.

Teacher Directions:

- Ask students to discuss and respond to the following statements:
  - Everyone is smart in many ways.
  - We have certain activities and tasks that seem easier than others.
  - With hard work and practice, we can improve in any of the eight areas!

Order of Activities

I have used the following activities with hundreds of students over the years. I see a genuine excitement in students when they hear we are all smart in some way. Many school settings tend to celebrate the linguistically or mathematically inclined students as successful or advanced. These activities show students that there are many ways to be smart, gifted, and talented. Even if you can't do this in the first few weeks, it will be worth your time to fit it in sometime in the beginning of the year!

1. Use the People Search to find classmates' various interests/strengths.

2. Have students complete the Inventory. (Grades 4–12, page 68)

3. Share and discuss the Strengths and Attributes associated with each of the 8 areas. **Be sure to highlight we *all have all 8 areas*, but we tend to have three or four that feel easier or come naturally to us.

Learning Strengths People Search

Teacher Directions:

- Distribute the Learning Strengths People Search to students. Everyone needs a pencil.
- Explain that they will have _____ minutes to walk around the room and calmly exchange papers with classmates.
- They are allowed to sign their name in ONE box on anyone's paper.
- Once they have signed once, they should trade with another person.
- If you want to make it competitive, announce that the first person with all boxes filled will earn bonus points on a future assignment.
- After students take the Learning Strengths Inventory and discuss the 8 types of smarts, have them look at the People Search again and take turns guessing which of the 8 areas each student scored the highest based on the box they signed on the search form.

Additional Activities

- ✓ Have students (3–12) take the quiz at www.thrively.com to not only find their gifts, but also to have activities selected for them to do online based on their profile. Amazing, free site.
- ✓ Connect students' gifts to real-world scenarios via picture books, online videos, or TedTalks. Let them see you are interested and paying attention.
- ✓ Set up a SeeSaw account and have students take photos and upload pics or artifacts of them engaged with their gifts or talents. SeeSaw app is a free, online visual portfolio.
- ✓ Check out anything by Kid President, especially the book *Kid President's Guide to Being Awesome*.

AIM FOR AWESOME

10 Ways to be Awesome Every Day

> *If you want to be a world changer for people everywhere, be a day maker for the people right next to you! – Brad Montague & Robby Novak, Kid President*

By the end of week two, you have spent a lot of time getting to know students. You have identified hopes and dreams, recognized personal gifts, and established a culture of respect. In weeks three and four, you will focus on setting goals, having a growth mindset, and using personal data to grow and improve. Students need a lot of coaching on how to fail forward and change habits to help themselves be more successful.

Robby Novak, Kid President, co-wrote an entire book on 100 ways to be awesome! There are so many ways to use his ideas throughout the year. I've chosen a few of his and added a few of my own to the "Aim for Awesome: 10 Ways to Be Awesome Every Day" poster. Print and post it if it fits your classroom culture, or create your own list with your students after showing them his video on YouTube: "Kid President's Guide to Being Awesome."[7]

Learning Strengths People Search

I play a sport. _____	I read often. _____	I play an instrument. _____	I love animals. _____
I love to camp or hike. _____	I make friends easily. _____	I enjoy writing in a journal. _____	I love to do math. _____
I like all types of music. _____	I like to paint. _____	I like learning about flowers & plants. _____	I love to meet new people. _____
I am good at building things. _____	I can write poems easily. _____	I can pick up a new dance step quickly. _____	I do many things by counting. _____
Drawing is easy OR fun for me. _____	I like having time to think about things. _____	I like to spend time in nature. _____	I prefer to do work by myself. _____

Learning Strengths Inventory

Rank each set of activities from 1 to 8 where **1** is the **lowest** in time, preference, or talent and **8** is the **highest**.

(Each group should have a 1, 2, 3, 4, 5, 6, 7, and 8.)

I spend the most time:

_____ Participating in outdoor activities (h)

_____ Drawing or painting (b)

_____ Playing an instrument (f)

_____ Being with others (d)

_____ Writing poems, stories, or letters (a)

_____ Working with computers or doing science projects (c)

_____ Doing things by myself (e)

_____ Exercising or playing sports (g)

I learn best by:

_____ Talking to others (d)

_____ Tuning into rhythm, turning things into a song (f)

_____ Seeing or making a picture, map, or diagram of an idea (b)

_____ Practicing, moving around a lot, and doing physical things (g)

_____ Taking time to understand things by myself (e)

_____ Listening, reading, writing, or speaking to myself (a)

_____ Analyzing, explaining, and understanding why (c)

_____ Using my senses to make connections to the world around me (h)

I prefer to:

_____ Take objects apart and figure out how they work (c)

_____ Exercise, ride a bike, or be active with my body (g)

_____ Look at comics, art, or movies (b)

_____ Observe rocks, plants, or animals (h)

_____ Join clubs and social activities (d)

_____ Listen to music (f)

_____ Read a book (a)

_____ Think about myself, my life, and how I handle situations (e)

I am good at:

_____ Recognizing, remembering, humming, or singing songs (f)

_____ Understanding people, knowing and appreciating people (d)

_____ Talking, writing, or playing with language and words (a)

_____ Looking at things, drawing, using maps (b)

_____ Using my hands or body to make or do things (g)

_____ Identifying patterns in my environment (h)

_____ Constructing things, pulling them apart, or asking "why" (c)

_____ Being myself, doing things at my own initiative and pace (e)

Profile: To score, add up the numbers for each letter and put the number next to the skill it represents. The highest number indicates the area in which you have the greatest interest or skill, or spend the most time and energy. The lowest numbers indicate the areas in which you have the least interest or current skill, and spend the least amount of time and energy.

a. Word Smart _____   **c. Logic Smart** _____   **e. Self Smart** _____   **g. Body Smart** _____

b. Picture Smart _____   **d. People Smart** _____   **f. Music Smart** _____   **h. Nature Smart** _____

People who are strongly:	Think/Learn	May Enjoy or Prefer	Benefit From
Linguistic – Word Smart	In words	Reading, writing, telling stories, playing word games, etc.	Books, tapes, writing tools, paper diaries, dialogues, discussion, debate, stories
Logical/ Mathematical – Logic Smart	By reasoning	Experimenting, questioning, figuring out puzzles, calculating, etc.	Things to explore and think about, science materials, manipulatives, trips to the planetarium and science museum
Spatial – Picture Smart	In images and pictures	Designing, drawing, visualizing, doodling, etc.	Art, LEGOs®, videos, movies, slides, imagination games, mazes, puzzles, illustrated books, trips to art museums
Bodily/ Kinesthetic – Body Smart	Through movement and physical engagement	Dancing, running, jumping, building, touching, gesturing, etc.	Role play, drama, movement, things to build, sports and physical games, tactile experiences, hands-on learning
Musical – Music Smart	Via rhythms and melodies	Singing, whistling, humming, tapping feet and hands, listening, etc.	Sing-along time, trips to concerts, music playing at home and school, musical instruments
Interpersonal – People Smart	By communicating with other people	Leading, organizing, relating, manipulating, mediating, partying, etc.	Friends, group games, social gatherings, community events, clubs, mentors/apprenticeships
Intrapersonal – Self Smart	Deeply inside themselves	Setting goals, meditating, dreaming, being quiet, etc.	Secret places, time alone, self-paced projects, choices
Naturalist – Nature Smart	About humans' impact on and with nature	Caring for animals, being outside, classifying plants/ flowers, camping, discovering things in nature	Time outside, books and shows about nature or animals, classroom plants or pets to care for, conservation or community-based projects, class garden

Aim for Awesome:
10 Ways to Be Awesome Every Day

Give 5 people a high five, low five, virtual five, or fist bump.

Celebrate today!
Every breath is a big deal.

Invent special glasses that help you only see things that are awesome.

Listen more than you talk.

Say something nice to yourself 3 times every day.

TREAT EVERYBODY LIKE IT'S THEIR BIRTHDAY.

Complain less.

Say "Thank you," "Excuse me," and "I'm sorry."

Sacrifice something you want for someone else.

BE YOURSELF.
EVERYBODY ELSE IS ALREADY TAKEN.

Illustrations courtesy of Vecteezy.com.

Adapted from Kid President's Guide to Being Awesome

Building Connections and Confidence
Chapter 2 Roadmap (Planning Guide)

Activity Choose one from each section	Action Items: What do you need to complete?	Date: When do you plan to use?	Page #
GETTING TO KNOW YOUR COMMUNITY			
Share Your Favorites			
Two Lies and a Truth			
10 in 10			
Stand at the Door			
Question of the Day			
Guess the Number			
Pick Your Greeting			
Are You Ready?			
Roll and Tell			
Where Would You Go?			
Rock, Paper, Scissors			
What is Your Favorite _____?			
Whiteboard Wisdom			
CELEBRATE STUDENTS' GIFTS			
Meet the Experts Board			
Meet the Experts Student Card			
Meet the Experts Presentations			
Gifts Gallery and "I'll Be Me" Poem			
Personal Bio Bag Project/All About Me			
Learning Strengths People Search			
Learning Strengths Inventory			
Have Students Take Thrively.com Quiz			
Set Up a SeeSaw Account			
AIM FOR AWESOME			
Share Kid President YouTube, Quotes, Book			
Hang Up "10 Ways to be Awesome" Poster			

CHAPTER THREE

Prevention, Procedures, and a Positive Approach to Discipline

A PREVENTION AND PROCEDURES

B CLASSROOM DISCIPLINE CYCLE

C CELL PHONE MANAGEMENT STRATEGIES

The number one problem in the classroom is not discipline; it is the lack of procedures and routines. – Harry Wong

 A **PREVENTION AND PROCEDURES**

Prevention is KEY

Establishing a positive classroom community is our number one goal at the start of the year. What they see and *feel* from day one will help students decide if your classroom is a place where they feel welcome, safe, and included, which determines whether they want to give their best effort. In addition to laying the groundwork for strong relationships and community, there must also be a commitment to teaching procedures and routines from day one to prevent problems. When we frontload skills, we set students up for success because they know not only *what* is expected but *how* to meet those expectations.

As I shared in Chapter 4 of *Behavior Interventions*, the tricky part is finding balance between teaching procedures and routines while also trying to get to know your students and make them feel welcome and excited. We can carefully prepare our agenda and activities for the first few weeks of school to ensure every student knows three things:

> 1. **Where they stand.**
> 2. **The teacher will follow through.**
> 3. **The teacher is on their side.**

1. Most students have a powerful need to know where they stand.

This means that adult expectations do not vary from day to day or student to student. Consistency and predictability may be absent in their personal lives, so it is critical for their sense of safety that we provide both in our classrooms. This chapter includes a list of procedures that should be directly taught to prevent common problems.

I've heard many comments from adults, especially when working with older students, such as "You should know better," or "I shouldn't have to tell you this." My response to that is, why? If you personally haven't taught them something you think is important, how can you know they know it? Developing a procedure manual and teaching lessons during warm-up or as a "bell ringer" every day for the first four weeks was an absolute game changer for me. I refer to these daily mini-lessons as "Procedure Boot Camp."

2. The teacher will follow through.

Students need to know the teacher can be trusted to take care of problems in a firm, fair, and respectful way. Students will accept consequences; they will not accept disrespect. If we tell a student that we will do something, we *must do it*! Students, and their caregivers, need to know that the teacher will follow through and will be consistent on how they follow through. This predictability creates a safe, calm classroom environment.

3. The teacher is on their side.

The single most common complaint I have heard from "challenging" kids throughout my career is, "That teacher doesn't like me." It does not even matter that their statement is untrue; their perception is their reality. Students need to feel like we are willing to listen, we want to help, and ultimately that we are on their side.

> **NOTE:** It may feel oversimplified, but using "please" and "thank you" when correcting students is extremely impactful if you want them to believe you are on their side. Some adults disagree with me on this, but I have found it to be effective in gaining compliance from a student when I make requests.

Procedure Boot Camp

I visit approximately 200 classrooms per year to provide support and coaching to K–12 teachers. I have a feedback form that I use so I can leave specific notes with ideas to solve problems. I love this part of my job because I get to offer solutions to the most common, and most annoying, behavior challenges teachers everywhere are facing.

One of the strategies I share often is how to have a Reboot Meeting with students. The meeting is held to identify what has gone wrong and to create a plan to correct it. Implementing your own Procedure Boot Camp is the main practice that will prevent the need to constantly reboot! Use the following ideas to plan which procedures you want to teach and the order in which you will teach them.

I highly suggest using the "5 Steps to Teach Anything" (Tell, Show, Practice, Feedback, Review) to teach your students the procedures. If "telling" children what to do was enough, you might not see an adult yell ever again!

- Entering the Classroom
- Warm-Up/Morning Work
- Call to Attention Signal (extremely important)
- Student Hand Raising
- Lining Up/Hallway Transitions (PreK–5)
- In-Class Transitions
- When I Don't Have a Pencil

1. Entering the Classroom

How students enter the room for the first time each day will set the tone for their effort, behavior, and interactions for the rest of the time they are there. The routine or lack of routine for the first five minutes is an indicator of a teacher's effectiveness overall. I have witnessed many students who quietly walk into one classroom, sit down, and work, only to burst into the very next class period and disrupt and destroy. The two most common reasons for this Jekyll and Hyde behavior? Lack of connection and lack of consistency in routines.

- Please enter with Level One voice.
- Greet your teacher and/or classmates.
- Sit in your seat.
- Begin your warm-up as soon as the bell rings.
- Check the "What to Do in the First 5" list for next steps.

What to Do in the First 5 (**This is a poster worth wall space!)

- Please enter with Level One voice.
- Please sit in your seat.
- Begin your warm-up as soon as the bell rings.
- Submit or file your warm-up.
- Read today's agenda. Make note in your agenda/calendar as needed.
- Write in your Table of Contents.
- Find your homework if assigned. Make sure it's complete.
- Read or study until the timer ends.

2. Warm-Up/Morning Work

I recommend using the same routines for opening work every day of the year. This consistency will start the day/class off calmly so instructional minutes are not wasted with constant verbal reminders and requests for quiet. Post the warm-up question/activity in the same place using the same format each day. You can mix up how you present, review, or discuss for variety, but posting it in the same way/place every day will help eliminate confusion. Example:

- Take out your Weekly Warm-up sheet (or go to Warm-up in Google classroom).
- Complete your warm-up before the timer ends.
- File in your binder/submit to teacher.
- Check the "What to Do in the First 5" list for next steps.

3. Call to Attention Signal/Call to Silence

This is the answer to the most common issue I see in classrooms everywhere I visit. Teachers are unable to get their students to stop talking. There are many creative options for this procedure. Choose one or two from the list that you will teach on day one and practice every day for three weeks. This procedure must be your most consistent during the first month or you will be pleading and fussing about the noise level all year.

- **Call and Repeat** –Teacher says a phrase; class responds with a phrase and then gets silent with eyes on the teacher. When the class meets your expectations, **PLEASE NOTICE IT!** ("I appreciate the quick attention.")

  ### Options: Pick One – Teacher Phrase/Student Response

  - Peanut Butter/Jelly Time
  - Don't Stop/ Get it, Get it

- We are awesome! / WE ARE AWESOME!
- Class, Class/Yes, Yes (Check out a compilation of many teachers using this whole-brain teaching strategy at https://tinyurl.com/yamps9e2)
- 1-2-3 Eyes on Me / 1-2, Eyes on You
- Count backward ("In 5-4-3-2-1")
- If you hear my voice clap once (clap) / If you hear my voice clap 2 times (clap, clap)
- What is 3 times 3? / 9! (continue with facts until all are silent)

• **NonVerbal Cue/Sign**

  - Hold up 5 fingers and wait.
  - Hold a closed hand and say, "Code O, please."
  - Use a bell, doorbell, or other noise maker.

• **Voice Levels/Code System**

Teach several voice levels so you can use specific language about student volume instead of saying "shhhh" or "be quiet." Those words mean different things to different people. Model the volume you are requesting, then ask students to practice each voice level multiple times throughout the first weeks. When a student is too loud, try, "Can you please take your voice to a Level One?" or "Level One voice, please. Thank you."

  - Code 0 – Silence. Eyes on speaker.
  - Code 1 – Speak to teacher only.
  - Code 2 – Speak to partner.
  - Code 3 – Speak to members of your group.

• **Countdown for Directions**

This strategy is simple but very effective in getting the entire class to follow directions at the same time. This also helps the teacher slow down and refrain from giving four or five directives in rapid-fire succession, which causes great stress to students who need more time to process what they hear. If you have more than two directives, use this strategy, but I also recommend the directions be in writing.

  - Give one direction at a time and count backward from 10 out loud for all students to hear.
  - Walk around the room and give positive feedback for students who have completed the request or are attempting to do it during the countdown.
  - You can give four directions and have the whole class finish in less than 1 minute.
  - Example: Please take out your notebook 10-9-8-7-6-5-4-3-2-1.

    Write your name on your paper 10-9-8-7-6-5-4-3-2-1. Thank you, now I need you to open the article on page ____ 10-9-8-7-6-5-4-3-2-1.

What to Do in the First 5

✓ Please enter with Level One voice.

✓ Please sit in your seat.

✓ Begin your warm-up as soon as the bell rings.

✓ Submit or file your warm-up.

✓ Read today's agenda.
Make note in your agenda/calendar as needed.

✓ Write in your Table of Contents.

✓ Find your homework, if assigned.
Make sure it's complete.

✓ Read or study until the timer ends.

CODE 0

Silence.
Eyes on speaker.

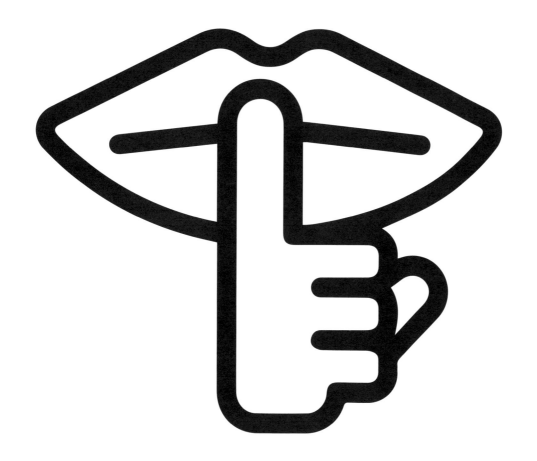

CODE 1

Speak to teacher only.

CODE 2

Speak to Partner.

CODE 3

Speak to members of your group.

4. Student Hand Raising

When asked to list the top three classroom behavior concerns by poll, teachers have overwhelmingly listed blurting out as number one or two. Every grade level, every age group, everywhere! A few simple preventative techniques can help you keep the blurting to a minimum while also providing multiple opportunities for students to talk and respond in a manageable way. Please remember, in every other aspect of their lives where they speak to people or have conversation, they are never required to raise their hands. It is a hard habit to develop!

- **Raise your own hand in the air.** Simple, but effective. Many students process what they see faster than what they hear. Teach students, "If my hand goes up, your hand goes up, and please wait to be called."

- **"Raise your hand to tell me..."** If you consistently preface every single question with these six words, you will eliminate most unwanted blurt-outs.

- **"Thank you for the raised hand."** Say this every single time you call on a student who has raised their hand. By saying the words both before and after, you are reminding them multiple times per day. Whatever you pay attention to, you will get more of it.

- **Wave an open hand in front of you from left to right.** Teach students that this means *anyone can call out an answer*. This is a structured, nonverbal cue that lets them know when you want an answer from whole-group response versus one person at a time. There are many times throughout the day where we allow and prefer the open-floor dialogue. If you don't have a specific cue, how will your students know when it's okay to blurt and when it is not?

5. Lining Up/Hallway Transitions (PreK–5)

Most elementary schools have expectations about walking around the school in a line. I have observed hundreds if not thousands of lines of students in my career. I want to address the one mistake I see more than any other. If there are 25 students in a class, and 23 are in a line, most teachers will speak to the two students who are not in line. I cannot express how important it is to speak to those who are meeting expectations first. Here are the most effective approaches I have used and observed:

- **Line them up quickly.** If you put students in a line, and they stand there for several minutes without moving, they *will* touch each other. The end.
  - Dismiss only a few at a time to get into the line.
  - Have a chosen line leader, or they will push and argue about it.
  - Remind them of expectations: "I am looking for safe hands, safe feet, and silent voices."
  - NOTICE STUDENTS WHO ARE MEETING EXPECTATIONS before you speak to anyone not meeting expectations.
- **Give the students a goal.** Tell them, "Our goal is to get to ___ with no more than two disruptions or with all hands to themselves." If they meet the goal, recognize them in your class reinforcement system.
- **Give fun ways to walk** – For primary grades, students love to walk like a ninja, walk on clouds, walk on tippy toes, etc.
- **Use a "Love the Line" sign when walking down the hall.** Flash it when you see expectations being met. Flip it over to "Check yourself, please" when students need to improve.

Love the line!

Check your line, please!

6. In-Class Transitions

Many teachers take for granted that students know how to move around the room in a safe, orderly way. The reason that so many students seem not to know is that each of their teachers has had different procedures. Spend time explaining how you want them to move safely around the classroom and have them practice the movement daily for the first few weeks. Remember to give that feedback each time!

Tips to help manage transitions:

- **Visual Timers** – www.classroomscreen.com has a timer and stopwatch tool
- **YouTube** – hundreds of timers with or without music
- **Timed Music Clips** – Play 30 seconds to one minute of the same song for the same transition each day. Students will get used to being in place before the song ends (nonverbal cueing).
- **3-2-1 Move** – This transition or dismissal strategy is simple. Teacher says:
    - On 3, all students clean their area.
    - On 2, students stand and push in their chairs.
    - On 1, students move to the next assigned area.

7. When I Don't Have a Pencil

There are many solid reasons students may not have the supplies they need. Most teachers attempt to stock up and purchase pencils on sale, but we still run out. Here are some ideas to help you manage "Pencil Gate."

- **Swap for Collateral** – Students must turn in an item that they truly want back to borrow a pencil for the agreed-upon time frame and then return the pencil/pen to retrieve got their personal item. I did this for years, and it was 95 percent effective in getting the borrowed materials back.
- **Numbered Pencils** – Assign a student to be the Pencil Assistant. Number a class set of pencils with a sharpie. Each day, the PA will hand out the same numbered pencil to the same student. If Josh is in the #14 desk, Josh receives the #14 pencil daily. The pencils are taken up each day and stored in the classroom.

> **Cause I Ain't Got a Pencil**
> By Joshua T. Dickerson
>
> I woke myself up
> Because we ain't got an alarm clock
> Dug into a dirty clothes basket
> Cause ain't nobody washed my uniform
> Brushed my hair and teeth in the dark
> Cause the lights ain't on
> Even got my baby sister ready
> Cause my mama wasn't home
> Got us both to school on time
> to eat us a good breakfast
> Then when I got to class the teacher fussed
> Cause I ain't got a pencil

DIY numbered pencil block - credit ETSY.com

3-2-1 Move

On 3...
all students
clean their area.

On 2...
students stand and
push in their chairs.

On 1...
students move to
the next assigned area.

Classroom Consequence System

Classroom management isn't about having the right rules;
it's about having the right relationships. – *Danny Steele @steelethoughts*

CLASSROOM DISCIPLINE CYCLE

Educators know it is so important to have a consistent and proactive plan for discipline. Many of us have struggled through classes we felt we could not manage; it is not fun at all. If you have spent time getting to know your students, building trust, and fostering community, most will usually accept discipline—especially if it is done with consistency and compassion. Having expectations and a plan that is **visible and clearly explained** is vital for maintaining the trust and a sense of fairness even when consequences must be issued. When discipline feels consistent, and students know the teacher will follow through, you will have fewer issues. It must be said that there will always be students for whom this, or any system, does not seem to deter inappropriate behavior. Chapter 7 focuses on more individualized options to try prior to becoming reliant on administrative intervention.

The Classroom Discipline Cycle is an effective and systematic way to communicate your classroom expectations with students, parents, and administration, track minor behaviors, and provide feedback and corrective consequences.

Introducing the System to Students

Every teacher will have a different view on when to introduce their classroom discipline system to students, but I have typically reviewed this with students at the end of week one or beginning of week two. It is not necessary to begin the school year and teacher/student relationship with discussions of what happens when it all goes wrong. **I also think it is important to introduce your positive behavior tracking system at the same time or on the same day as the CDC.** We want students to understand that the teacher will be noticing positive behaviors as often if not more than we notice behaviors that don't meet expectations.

- Share with the class that to meet community agreements and keep everyone safe, you will respond to both positive and negative behaviors.
- I like to directly state that they will get more attention for positive choices than they will for disruptive choices.
- Show the CDC poster and explain how the reminders will work (see explanation below).
- Share the reflection form, and let them know that the first two times they receive one, it will be placed in a folder with no further consequences so they have plenty of opportunities to work out their choices.
- Talk about the consequences of positive choices (left side of menu) and possible consequences of poor choices.
- Allow students to ask questions.

Reminder System

REMINDER #1

Nonverbal Warning

Here are three examples of common nonverbal cues:

- The "look" – making eye contact and nodding or using another gesture
- Proximity Control – moving next to student and standing briefly to encourage
- Correction Cards – printed notes that clearly state your request.

Demonstrate how you will use each of these cues and have students role play and practice their response.

Correction Cards

These are small, laminated index cards or cardstock cards that have corrective statements printed on them. These are used as a nonverbal reminder of the expected behavior. In the classroom discipline cycle, these are used as my Reminder One/Nonverbal warning. Choose the card that best fits the corrective statement you would like to make.

Teacher Directions:

- Place the card on the student's desk who needs the reminder and keep moving. NO verbal feedback to student.
- Each card should have the number 2 on the back before laminating.
- Flip the card over to show the "2" when you need to follow up with a verbal reminder (Reminder 2.)

REMINDER #2

Verbal Warning

Using a sentence frame to verbally address classroom behaviors is an excellent way to establish consistency and trust. If all students are corrected in the same manner, it will reduce feelings on "that's not fair" and increase respect. You can use this sentence as an independent intervention or pair it with correction cards.

If you need to correct a student a second time, walk over to the student, flip the correction card over to the back to show the number 2 which means 2nd chance. This is a "last chance" reminder that lets the student know the next disruptive behavior will result in a consequence. When you turn it over, try to get eye level and to the side of the student, and quietly say, **"If you choose to continue _____, you choose ____."**

Teacher Examples:

- If you choose to continue talking, you choose to move your seat.
- If you choose to use that language in my room, you choose to speak to _____ (fill in person).
- If you choose not to do your work during class, you choose to do it at home or in academic support time as a working lunch.

NOTE: When you correct behavior, make every effort to also give specific positive feedback to two or more students who are meeting expectations. Every time! It creates a culture of positivity when we notice what's right more than we notice what's wrong. A positive classroom community of learners is the goal!

Thanks for your silence.

Thanks for staying on task.

Thank you for following directions.

Thank you for staying in your seat.

Correction Cards #1

Teacher Directions:

Print, cut out, fold in half, and laminate several copies of each correction card. Carry them on a clipboard or central location for easy accessibility. Place in front of student as a nonverbal reminder. Take it up after 15 minutes or at the end of a class period – your choice.

Thank you for staying in your seat.

Thank you for staying in your seat.

Thank you for staying in your seat.

Correction Cards #2

Teacher Directions:

Print, cut out, fold in half, and laminate several copies of each correction card. Carry them on a clipboard or central location for easy accessibility. Place in front of student as a nonverbal reminder. Take it up after 15 minutes or at the end of a class period – your choice.

 **Thank you for staying on task.**

 **Thank you for staying on task.**

 **Thank you for staying on task.**

Correction Cards #3

Teacher Directions:

Print, cut out, fold in half, and laminate several copies of each correction card. Carry them on a clipboard or central location for easy accessibility. Place in front of student as a nonverbal reminder. Take it up after 15 minutes or at the end of a class period – your choice.

Thank you for your silence.

Thank you for your silence.

Thank you for your silence.

Correction Cards #4

Teacher Directions:

Print, cut out, fold in half, and laminate several copies of each correction card. Carry them on a clipboard or central location for easy accessibility. Place in front of student as a nonverbal reminder. Take it up after 15 minutes or at the end of a class period – your choice.

Please stop. Thank you.

Please stop. Thank you.

Please stop. Thank you.

REMINDER # 3:

Consequence Menu

The bottom of the CDC poster includes a menu or a variety of classroom-level consequences from which the teacher will choose, based on student behavior and frequency of behavior. Common corrective actions on a classroom consequence menu are working lunch, loss of privilege, think time in or out of the classroom, or parent contact. Most of the options on the consequence menu are classroom level consequences and should be managed by the teacher.

Reflection Form/Better Choices Sheet

The Better Choices Sheet is a reflection form that serves as documentation for the teacher when a student has received a consequence. This form can serve as the consequence, especially for the first or second time a student has reached the limit of reminders.

If it is the third time (or more) that a student has reached the limit and now needs a consequence such as parent contact, working lunch, time out, etc., the student should fill out the form in addition to the consequence. This creates a paper trail for the teacher to be able to show all that has been tried without outside support. It also, more importantly, serves as a reflection for the student so they can begin to think of ways to do better in the future.

If a student refuses to fill out the form, DO NOT ARGUE OR REACT. I suggest using this phrase: "You can fill it out in your words, or I will fill it out for you; it's your choice." If they refuse to fill it out, you can let them know that you will fill it out and must make note that the student refused to fill out the form. I want to share that I say these statements in a very flat, low voice. I have found it is much more effective in keeping communication positive as well as helps me not to lose my cool!

Here is how the "Pink Slips" add up from minors to a major (office referral):

1st slip – Fill out pink slip/discuss with student/file only;

2nd – Fill out pink slip/discuss with student/file only;

3rd – Fill out pink slip/parent contact/consequence from the menu;

4th – Fill out pink slip/parent contact/consequence requiring more time;

5th – Office referral – all others after 5th also result in office referrals IF your administration approves this.

NOTE: These numbers can be modified in any way that fits your classroom/student needs. I have seen several variations of this system that have worked well.

Reflection Form/Pink Slip

Name: _____

Date: _____

This is what I did: _____

_____ .

I did that because: _____

_____ .

This is how I felt:

| Sad | Tired | Confused | Happy | Frustrated |

Next time I will: _____

_____ .

Think Sheet (Gr K-2)

How are you feeling?

Happy   Sad   Frustrated

Scared   Silly   Excited

Surprised   Shy/Quiet   Embarrassed

What happened?

What can you do differently next time?

How do you feel now?

Better Choices Sheet

Name:_____ Date:_____Time:_____

My actions (What I did): _____

_____

_____

_____.

Next time, I can choose to:_____

_____

_____

_____.

The reason I made the wrong choice is: _____

_____

_____

_____.

To help myself next time something like this happens, I will: _____

_____

_____

_____.

Student Signature: _____

Teacher/ Adult: _____

Better Choices Sheet

Name: _____

Date: _____ Time: _____

My actions (What I did): _____
_____
_____

Next time, I can choose to: _____
_____
_____

The reason I made the wrong choice is: _____
_____
_____

To help myself next time something like this happens, I will: _____
_____
_____

Student Signature: _____

Teacher/ Adult: _____

Better Choices Sheet

Name: _____

Date: _____ Time: _____

My actions (What I did): _____
_____
_____

Next time, I can choose to: _____
_____
_____

The reason I made the wrong choice is: _____
_____
_____

To help myself next time something like this happens, I will: _____
_____
_____

Student Signature: _____

Teacher/ Adult: _____

Self-Reflection Journal

Weekly Goal:	
Date:	I met my goal: ☐ YES ☐ NO

Did you follow directions appropriately? ☐ YES   ☐ NO

What was your behavior? _____

_____

_____

What did you want? (put a check next to the appropriate statement)

☐   I wanted attention from others.

☐   I wanted to be in control.

☐   I wanted to avoid doing my homework.

☐   I created conflict because I am sad inside.

☐   I created conflict because they don't like me.

Did you get what you wanted? ☐ YES   ☐ NO

What could you do differently? _____

_____

Goal for next week: _____

_____

Apology Slip

The Apology Slip is used when I see or overhear a student do something mean or hurtful to someone else. This is for minor name calling, disrespecting others' property, and non-physical/non-threatening things that don't yet warrant an office referral but do warrant a reaction from the teacher. The student fills out the Apology Slip, and the teacher files it. I suggest allowing two "free passes" per school year. Once a student receives a third slip, a parent contact and referral to a counselor is the consequence. I do the same thing for each time beyond the third Apology Slip.

Apology Slip

Name:_____ Date:_____ Name of person harmed: _____

This is what I did: _____

_____

_____

What I should have done was: _____

_____

_____

When I harmed_____, I think they felt_____

_____

_____

I would like to say: _____

_____

_____

Signed (Student completing the form): _____

Signed (Adult): _____

Comments: _____

_____

_____

Letter to Parents about Classroom Systems

Our students' parents and caregivers play a vital role in their education and the success of your classroom. We want to reach out to them early and often to share expectations and intentions. Just as students need to feel welcome, safe, and included, their parents want to know what you will do to ensure those three needs are met daily. You will find a sample letter below that gives a lot of detail about your classroom systems. I suggest you send it home, review it during any open house event, and post it on your website or E-classroom so parents can easily access it. Please be sure to have your administrator review and approve any communication about discipline before you share.

Sample Parent Letter

Dear Parents and Caregivers,

Thank you for partnering with me to make this a positive, successful year of learning and personal growth for your student. I would like to share how I will celebrate and correct your student's choices in our classroom. First, we will be using _____ (Dojo, class tickets, Teacher/Student scoreboard, etc.) to recognize positive choices students make. It is my belief that it is more important to notice the positive behaviors first and more often than noticing negative behaviors. I will communicate with you regularly on the amazing things I know your student will be doing. Here are ways your student may be celebrated throughout the year:

- High Fives, Hand Claps, Cheers
- Dojo Points
- Positive Note/Call Home
- Personal Sticky Note

- Student of the Week
- MVP or VIP Desk
- Verbal Affirmation
- Bonus Privilege Opportunities (Fun Stuff!)

I also want you to know that I plan to address the not-so-great choices in our classroom in a caring, consistent manner. I will only call on you for support if a behavior is dangerous, or minor but repetitive and I am not seeing changes. The approach I use for correcting behavior is called the Classroom Discipline Cycle. This is the system I use to manage and minimize minor behavior incidents. All students may receive three reminders/redirections when causing a disruption or making a poor choice. These include:

Reminder 1 - NonVerbal Warning

Reminder 2 - Verbal Warning

Reminder 3 - Consequence Menu (Teacher Discretion)

- Reflection Form (to think and plan)
- Teacher Discussion
- Opportunity to Repair/Restore
- Loss of privilege
- Last to Leave or Line Up
- Working lunch (Parent/Caregiver notified)
- Think Time in another classroom for ___ minutes (Parent/Caregiver notified)
- Behavior Contract (Parent/Caregiver call & part of the planning)

After **four** Reflection Forms have been issued for minor behavior incidents, an office referral will be written. Caregivers will be contacted every time after the 2nd Reflection Form, as I want your student to have a few opportunities to reflect and correct their own behavior before you are called. Please contact me with any questions, and I look forward to working together to make this a great year!

Sincerely,

Classroom Discipline Cycle Template

Teacher Directions :

- Add your classroom expectations at the top (numbered 1-3, but you can add up to 5).
- Think about each of the three sections of your Classroom Discipline Cycle.
- What will you use for your reminders?
- What are the positive consequences you choose to incorporate—list them all!
- What are the corrective consequences that are a possibility in your classroom that align with your school/administration's expectations and approval?

Classroom Discipline Cycle (CDC)

1.

2.

3.

Classroom Disruptions Will Result on a Reminder

Reminder 1 =

Reminder 2 =

Reminder 3 =

Positive Consequence Menu

Corrective Consequence Menu

CELL PHONE MANAGEMENT STRATEGIES

We are in a cell phone epidemic. I visit many middle and high school classrooms around the country, and this is a huge battle for educators. I have seen a few ideas that are helping teachers combat the lost instructional minutes and constant distractions that cell phones in the classroom can cause.

1. Cell Phone Drop

- Use a cloth or plastic shoe caddy.
- Number each pouch.
- Incorporate a Class Challenge for ___ days without a cell phone distraction.
- Include only a few chargers that will reach the phones while in the caddy as an added incentive for specific students with no infractions in your class.

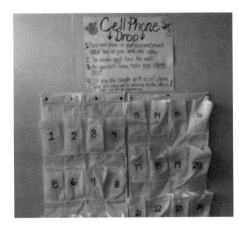

2. Cell Phone Charging Station

The idea of having a cell phone charging station comes with a cost, but some educators may find it worth it to keep cell phones in a centralized and organized space. Here is a great article with pictures and videos on multiple ways to DIY: https://scienceandliteracy.org/diy-chromebook-charging-station/

There are also multiple options online such as this charging port that can charge up to ten devices at the same time. This would also be an earned opportunity when students have followed the cell phone policy in your classroom. https://tinyurl.com/y9uoz5ox

3. Cell Phone "Detention"

This is a compromise when students have broken the cell phone policy. Use a crate or other see-through container for students to place their phones when they are caught using them during a "no cell phone" portion of class. The teacher agrees to use this as a "second chance" opportunity where a student can place the phone, see the phone, and get it back at the end of class. There is no charging option in cell phone detention. After the third infraction, the cell phone is given to an administrator.

4. Class Challenge – 10 Days of Excellence

After explaining your school's or your personal classroom cell phone policy, offer a group challenge to your class(es). The name of this challenge came from a teacher in Rockdale County, Georgia. Let your students know that you will be tracking each day of "excellence" on the chart per class period. You should decide if the ten days have to be consecutive or not. I suggest ten days at any pace/any time for this challenge. Once ten cell phone images are circled, the class earns a predetermined privilege, such as 15 minutes of tech time, 15 minutes of talk time, a set number of points on an assignment, or a free snack day where students can bring in any snacks to consume during the last half of class. Place the full-page Goal Tracker in a page protector so you can reuse it.

Cell Phone Drop Expectations

1. Please place your phone in your assigned number slot each day when you enter the room.

2. Please have your screen face the back of the pouch, and put on SILENT.

3. When you leave class, take ONLY YOUR PHONE.

4. If you have an emergency, you may request to use it in the first or last 3 minutes of class. You must have permission from the teacher.

**Every 10 days without any cell phone distractions = 1 day of cell phones for the last 15 minutes of class.

Cell Phone Contract

Student Name _____

1. Students may use cell phones before school, after school, and during break.

2. Students may not use cell phones ANY other time in this classroom.

3. Cell phones must be turned off and put away during class.

4. Failure to give your phone to school personnel is an act of defiance and may result in an office referral.

If a student is caught using a cell phone during class, the following will apply:

First Time: Cell phone will be taken away and put in cell phone detention area. The student may retrieve their phone at the end of the class after signing this contract.

Second Time: Cell phone will be taken away and student can retrieve their phone at the end of the day. Student will sign this contract.

Third Time: Cell phone will be taken away and turned in to an administrator.

Any further offense may result in loss of privilege to use a cell phone at school and will require a parent to pick up the phone.

_____   _____
Student Signature   First Time   Date

_____   _____
Student Signature   Second Time   Date

_____   _____
Parent Signature   Date

Please note: Cell phones are brought on campus at your own risk.
Lost, stolen, or damaged cell phones are not the responsibility of the school.

10 Days of Excellence

Block:_____

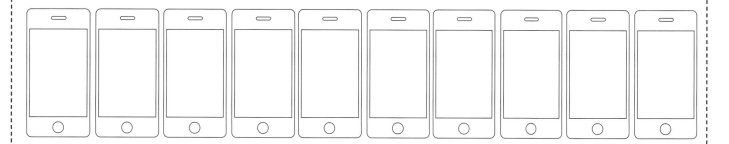

Once we have met 10 Days of Excellence, we will _____.

10 Days of Excellence

Block:_____

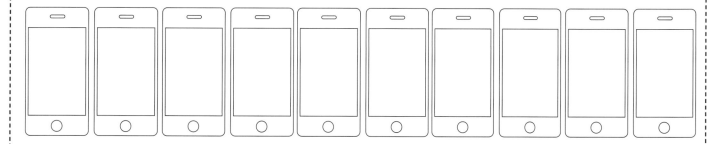

Once we have met 10 Days of Excellence, we will _____.

Prevention, Procedures, and a Positive Approach to Discipline
Chapter 3 Roadmap (Planning Guide)

Activity Choose 1 from each section	Action Items: What do you need to complete?	Date: When do you plan to use?	Page #
PREVENTION AND PROCEDURES			
What To Do in the First 5-Minutes of Class			
Call and Repeats			
Nonverbal Warning			
Voice Levels/Code System			
Countdown for Directions			
Student Hand Raising			
Lining Up/Hallway Transition			
Timers			
30-Second Song Clips			
3-2-1 Move			
Pencil Strategy			
CLASSROOM DISCIPLINE CYCLE			
Introducing the System to Students			
Reminder 1: Correction Cards			
Reminder 2: Verbal Warning			
Reminder 3: Consequence Menu			
Reflection Form/Better Choices Sheet			
Apology Slip			
Letter to Parents			
Classroom Discipline Cycle			
CELL PHONE MANAGEMENT STRATEGIES			
Cell Phone Drop			
Cell Phone Contract			
Cell Phone Charging Station			
Cell Phone "Detention"			
10 Days of Excellence			

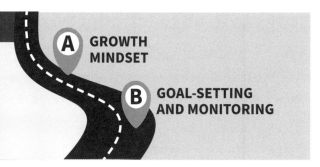

CHAPTER FOUR

Growth Mindset, Goal-Setting, and Monitoring

A **GROWTH MINDSET**

B **GOAL-SETTING AND MONITORING**

*The future belongs to those who believe
in the beauty of their dreams. – Eleanor Roosevelt*

 GROWTH MINDSET

What Is Growth Mindset?

Carol Dweck, a Stanford University psychology professor, spent decades researching the idea that people have the ability to develop and expand their own mental capacity in order to learn at more advanced levels based on the way they *think* about learning.

This powerful concept is referred to as *growth mindset*. People with a growth mindset believe that their brain is constantly evolving and able to learn new things. People with a *fixed mindset* do not believe that their skills can be improved, and studies have shown they are less likely to be successful because of negative self-talk.

As educators, we are often tasked with the difficult job of closing academic achievement gaps. This challenge becomes even more difficult when we teach students who are stuck in a fixed mindset and tell themselves or others, "I can't do this."

After spending three weeks building community, establishing routines and procedures, and identifying all the wonderful ways students will contribute to your class this year, you can introduce growth mindset and goal setting in week four. This is the perfect time to ask students to consider what academic or personal growth goals they want to focus on for the year. I recommend teaching them how to set, track, and monitor their goals so they can modify and adapt on the way to achievement.

You will find multiple activities and forms that you can use with students over several days or weeks to set up your Finish Line Friday folders. The tools will help them reflect and plan throughout the year with personal goal setting and progress monitoring. I have included forms you can print and share or use them for inspiration to create or find something that best fits your needs.

Books to Read to Introduce Growth Mindset

We love a good read-aloud to kick off a classroom conversation or new concept we want students to learn. I read *The Dot*, by Peter Reynolds, every year in my secondary classrooms to introduce the Power of Yet—one of my favorite things to teach students of all ages!

Growth Mindset Activities

The following ideas are intended for K–12 classrooms as activities to use to help students understand growth mindset, build confidence in themselves, and develop a "I can do hard things" attitude. Although there are several options listed here, I suggest choosing one or two to use that fits the age and needs of your students. Have fun!

1. Growth Mindset—Make Big Goals Happen

> **Teacher Directions:**
>
> Distribute or display the Growth Mindset—Make Big Goals Happen page for students. Discuss the two types of thinking that were discovered and researched by Dr. Carol Dweck. Ask students to share examples of times they pushed through something hard and achieved it, as well as a time when they have given up on something or found something frustrating. Once students have an understanding of growth versus fixed mindset, choose an activity for students to complete once a week for a few weeks or as needed. You could also create a Growth Mindset Stations activity where students move through and experience each of the following activities.

GROWTH MINDSET
Make Big Goals Happen!

LEARNS FROM FAILURE

KEEPS GOING

PUTS IN EFFORT

EMBRACES CHALLENGES

LEARNS FROM FEEDBACK

GROWTH
MINDSET

IGNORES FEEDBACK

DOESN'T TRY

MISTAKES ARE BAD

GIVES UP EASILY

AVOIDS CHALLENGES

FIXED
MINDSET

2. Personal Achievements Timeline

Teacher Directions:

Distribute the Personal Achievements Timeline to students. Complete one for yourself so you can share an example of how to complete the timeline. Ask students to list major things they have learned to do in their lives by age or year (for example, learned to talk, walk, tie their shoes, climb a tree/monkey bars, ride a bike, write their name, read, play an instrument, hit a baseball, etc.). Explain that the time or date doesn't need to be exact—just a general age of when they learned to do it. Discuss how impossible these skills may have seemed before they learned to do them and practiced over time. Ask them how they overcame, persevered, and became the experts they are today with the accomplishments they chose to highlight.

3. Mindset Re-FRAME

Teacher Directions:

Distribute the Mindset Re-FRAME page and have students rewrite the negative self-talk as positive self-talk.

4. GRITS Notes

What are GRITS? These are notes that **Give Real Inspiration To Students**. Use these personal notes to give to students when you see them working hard, pushing through, and showing GRIT in your classroom!

Teacher Directions:

Explain to students that one of the most common attributes of successful people is working hard and pushing through challenges. This is called GRIT. Tell your students that you will be watching and listening for positive thinking, hard work when the work is hard, and a never-give-up attitude. You will hand out GRITS to students when you see their efforts.

5. Classroom Poster – Attitude of Gratitude

When we help students develop an attitude of gratitude, we are helping them create a conscious mindset and habit to be thankful for the big and small positives in their lives. This will help them focus on what they do well versus focusing on what they cannot do because they know how to turn a negative thought into a positive one.

Teacher Directions:

This list of positive self-talk is to help students focus on the things they are thankful for each day, so that the practice of positive thinking is accessible when challenges arise. You can post this in your classroom and make it a daily practice to read it out loud or use when needed.

Personal Achievement Timeline for _____

Directions: Fill in a few big achievements you've had or things you've learned to do. Share how you became good at each one.

Achievement: _____

Year: _____

How did you do it?
_____
_____
_____

Achievement: _____

Year: _____

How did you do it?
_____
_____
_____

Achievement: _____

Year: _____

How did you do it?
_____
_____
_____

Achievement: _____

Year: _____

How did you do it?
_____
_____
_____

Achievement: _____

Year: _____

How did you do it?
_____
_____
_____

Mindset Re-Frame

Directions: The frames on the left show the thoughts of a person with a fixed mindset using negative self-talk. Rewrite each thought as positive self-talk.

I am not good at this. I quit.	
The last time I tried this, I failed. It's a waste of my time to try again.	
I hate making mistakes.	
Everyone can do this except me.	
I'll never be good at math.	

GRITS Notes: Give Real Inspiration to Students

I noticed you didn't give up when you were frustrated. Keep it up!

You showed so much GRIT today! Incredible!

I noticed you tried several strategies to SOLVE the problem. Great effort!

I AM PROUD OF THE RISKS YOU TOOK TODAY. YOU ROCK!

YOUR BRAIN IS THE SUPER STAR OF THE DAY! HARD WORK PAYS OFF.

YOUR never-give-up attitude is an inspiration. Be proud of YOU!

Attitude of Gratitude

Always Have an Attitude of Gratitude

Sterling K. Brown

Every day, I am thankful that:
I am smart and capable.
I can do hard things.
I can learn and get better at anything with effort.
I am awesome.
I am here for a reason.
I am enough.

What else are you thankful for today?

PROS: Professionals in Training

In Chapter 1, you were asked to consider your big goals for your students. Were any of your goals related to their future? Is preparing them for their next step in life part of your plan? One of my big goals for students included preparing them for the world of work. Almost everything they are asked to do in school, K—12 and post-secondary, provides practice for the expectations they will experience in their future occupation.

Because I believe this so strongly, I created a framework in my classroom for teaching professionalism to my students. I used it with most of my classes for over ten years. This idea can be used at almost any grade level if the vocabulary and concepts are presented in a way that is accessible to your specific age group. One of the most beneficial outcomes of teaching the concept of PROS was that it also allowed for certain behaviors to be corrected without conveying judgment. Using PROS language allows you to address behavior in a way that is not based on opinions, history, or personal upbringing, but rather on a commonly accepted set of expectations that most employers will have of employees. Students of all ages can benefit from envisioning themselves doing a job that motivates them, and this taps into their hopes and dreams while sprinkling in some "real talk" and solid practice.

Teacher Directions:

Ask students for examples of people going to work or careers. Ask students what the word *professional* means. Explain to students that professionalism is the skill, knowledge, good judgment, and positive behavior it takes to do a job well. Let them know that every day they are in the class together, they are practicing for the job they hope to have one day. All students are PITs—or Professionals in Training—while they are in the classroom community. Using this language allows the teacher to make positive corrections by asking a student to show PRO behavior rather than "You shouldn't" and "That's inappropriate," comments about behaviors that don't help students know what to do to improve.

Examples:

- "The language we use in this classroom is the language we would use at work; can you try to say that in a way you would speak to your manager?"
- "What's another way you can tell your coworker (classmate) to leave you alone?"
- "I can see you are upset. How can we handle anger when we are in a work environment?"

Teacher Directions:

Distribute the PIT Every Day worksheet to students. Ask them to consider the different ways they show the characteristics of professionalism in their everyday lives.

PROFESSIONALS IN TRAINING
We Can All Be Pros!

Professional

- Dress for success
- Be on time
- Own your mistakes
- Work hard every day

Respectful

- Be polite (how you might talk to your grandmother)
- Respond when someone speaks to you
- Use calm words–even when upset

Organized

- Keep your area neat and organized
- Keep up with your agenda/calendar to help you remember
- Have only the materials you need in your space

Skilled

- Be confident, but not extra
- Become an expert in your job but continue to learn
- Always give 100%

There's No Dream Too Tall by Amie Dean   © National Center for Youth Issues   www.ncyi.org

Professionals in Training "PIT" Everyday Worksheet

Every day you go to school, YOU are a professional in training! You are practicing many of the skills you will need to be a successful professional. A ***professional*** is a person who has certain character traits while at work. We will focus on 5 traits you can practice every day so you will be ready for your future!

In the space provided after each trait, write one way YOU have shown that trait in your daily life.

1. Be Committed: _____

_____

(Ex. Show up & work hard. Be willing to listen and learn. Do what it takes to do a good job.)

2. Be Respectful: _____

_____

(Ex. Treat others with respect. Use kind words and language. Disagree by using "I" statements.)

3. Be Honest: _____

_____

(Ex. Tell the truth even when it is hard or scary. Do the right thing even if nobody is watching you.)

4. Be Responsible: _____

_____

(Ex. Show up on time and stay until the end. Do your tasks when you are asked. Give your BEST effort every time.)

5. Be a Problem-Solver: _____

_____

(Ex. If you find something is broken, try to fix it. Ask for help instead of saying, "I can't." Always try to see both sides of any problem.)

There's No Dream Too Tall by Amie Dean   © National Center for Youth Issues www.ncyi.org

Goal-Setting for Students

After discussing professionals and what they do, you can share that successful professionals, and successful students, set goals and track their progress toward those goals. A critical step in goal setting and tracking is *changing* your behavior or habits when your progress is not where you want it to be. It is a step that many students often miss or lack understanding of its impact on achievement.

Finish Line Friday Folders:

In week four or five, I suggest introducing Finish Line Fridays. You now have some student work samples and some data to be able to create Finish Line Friday folders for students.

- Give each student a folder.
- Students are encouraged to decorate their folders with goals, dreams, inspirational quotes, and pictures or words that are motivational to them personally.
- Each folder includes several documents they will use for the first nine weeks or semester (teacher's choice).
- One or two Fridays per month, folders are distributed, and students will review assignments, grades, and any other data points to monitor their progress.
- SeeSaw.com, Google Sheets, and LiveBinders.com are also paperless options for charting student data in 1:1 classrooms. Check this link to TpT for a pack of Google Sheets that are editable: https://tinyurl.com/yc2elblt.

Choose from the following tools to build and support student Finish Line Friday folders.

- SMART Goal Planning Form 1 or 2 (2–12) – guides students in setting/tracking goals
- Blank Goal-Graphing Form (K–12) – students can visually chart progress
- Student Growth Form (K–12) – tracks growth from pre-test to post-test for any learning goal
- Effort vs. Achievement Rubric (6–12) – requires students to self-assess effort
- Goal Celebration Cards (K–5)

SPECIFIC   MEASURABLE   ATTAINABLE   RELEVANT   TIME-BASED

SMART Goal Planning Form

Today's Date:_____   **Target Date:**_____

Start Date:_____   **Date Achieved:**_____

Goal: _____

Specific: What exactly will you accomplish? _____

_____

Measurable: How will you know when you have reached this goal?

_____

_____

Achievable: Is achieving this goal realistic with effort and commitment?
Do you have the resources to achieve this goal? If not, how will you get them?

_____

_____

Relevant: Why is this goal significant to your life?

_____

_____

Timely: When will you achieve this goal?

_____

_____

SMART Goal Planning Form

Name:_____

Directions: Use the SMART goals guide below to help plan your goals. Then write your goal at the top of the staircase and the steps you need to take to achieve it.

MY GOAL:

STEP 3

STEP 2

STEP 1

Create Smart Goals

S - Specific	What exactly do you want to accomplish?
M - Measureable	How will you know when your goal is met?
A - Attainable	What steps can you take to reach your goal?
R - Relevant	How will meeting this goal help you?
T - Time-Based	How long will it take you to reach your goal?

Goal-Graphing Form

Directions: Write the name of the task or assignment on the line at the bottom.
Shade or color up the row of blocks to show the score/grade you earned.

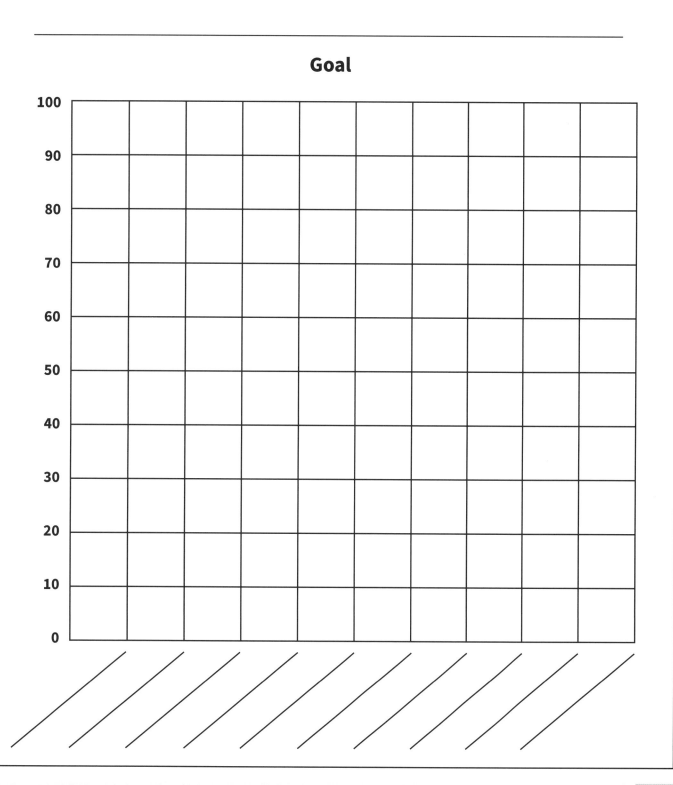

Goal

Student Growth Form

Name:_____ Class:_____

Activity	Pre-Test	Post-Test	Difference +/-

Effort vs. Achievement Rubric

EFFORT RUBRIC

4   I worked on the task until it was completed. I pushed myself to continue working on the task even when it was difficult. I viewed difficulties as opportunities to strengthen my understanding.

3   I worked on the task until it was completed. I pushed myself to continue working on the task even when it was difficult or a solution was not immediately evident.

2   I put some effort into the task, but I stopped working when difficulties arose.

1   I put very little effort into the task.

ACHIEVEMENT RUBRIC

4   I exceeded the objectives of the task or lesson. (Grade is an A.)

3   I met the objectives of the task or lesson. (Grade is a B.)

2   I met a few of the objectives of the task/lesson, but did not meet others. (Grade is a C.)

1   I did not meet the objectives of the task or lesson. (Grade is an F.)

Student scores self.

EFFORT AND ACHIEVEMENT CHART			
DATE:	ASSIGNMENT:	EFFORT:	ACHIEVEMENT:
8/21/22	Moon Phases	2	2

Goal Celebration Cards

Teacher Directions:

Choose the design that best fits your students and the message you want to convey. Send these cards home with students to celebrate and connect with families when a goal has been achieved. You may wish to include a note of congratulations or encouragement on the back of the card.

Growth Mindset, Goal-Setting, and Monitoring
Chapter 4 Roadmap (Planning Guide)

Activity Choose 1 from each section.	Action Items: What do you need to complete?	Date: When do you plan to use?	Page #
GROWTH MINDSET			
Which Book(s) Will You Read?			
Growth Mindset – Make Big Goals Happen!			
Personal Achievements Timeline			
Mindset Re-FRAME			
GRITS – Give Real Inspiration to Students			
Attitude of Gratitude Poster			
GOAL-SETTING AND M0NITORING			
PROS – Professionals in Training			
Finish Line Friday Folders			
SMART Goals Planning Forms			
Goal-Graphing Form			
Student Growth Form			
Effort vs. Achievement Rubric			
Goal Celebration Cards			

Keeping Your Community Strong – Activities to Use All Year

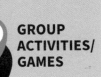

A COMMUNITY BUILDERS

B GROUP ACTIVITIES/ GAMES

The best feeling in the world is seeing the benefits and rewards of hard work.
– Kevin Hart – Actor, Comedian, Entrepreneur

 A **COMMUNITY BUILDERS**

Consistency is Key

Chapters 1 through 4 focused heavily on how to set up your positive classroom community in the first weeks of the school year. By week five or six, your students are likely settled in, procedures and routines have become habits, and if things are going well, most of your minutes are spent on instruction and student learning. You have worked hard to connect with your students, identify and celebrate their gifts, and create a space where they want to be.

Experienced educators also know this is often the time when the "honeymoon" period may be coming to an end. As students become more comfortable in the classroom, some begin to display behaviors that they worked hard to minimize in the beginning. Continuing to have brief, yet consistent, opportunities to ensure that students feel connected, capable, and calm is vital to preventing the behaviors that surface around this time.

This chapter highlights many ways to continue to focus on your classroom culture while also protecting vital minutes needed for student learning. There are two ideas that require a daily commitment that are typically a better match in elementary classrooms. You will find several more that take less time, but still make a big impact in building relationships and trust at all grade levels.

Daily Community Meetings (Grades K-5)

In all my years both teaching in and visiting classrooms, the single most effective practice for building relationships that I experienced was a daily morning meeting. I prefer to call this our community meeting, which can be done any time of the day. The start of the day is significant in preventing behaviors, as it helps students meet the 3 Cs first thing in the morning. Bringing students into a circle to start their day with their peers by checking in, sharing their thoughts or feelings, as well as getting focused attention from the teacher is the catalyst for a successful day for many students.

The purpose of the Community Meeting:

- Build a strong sense of connection and community
- Set the tone for the day and overall classroom climate
- Encourage teamwork, a growth mindset, and collaboration
- Support social-emotional needs for all students so academic learning and engagement can take place

Resources for Running a Daily/Community Meeting

The ideal meeting is 15-20 minutes each morning for the K–5 classroom, but any time between 10-25 minutes works if it's interactive and well managed. Before beginning, and in the first few days, I suggest the following:

- Inform parents that you will hold a daily morning meeting and share the purpose and outcomes.
- Tell students you will meet each day in a Community Meeting to get to know one another, build trust, and learn to communicate with classmates. Sometimes, you will use the meeting time to learn, solve problems or concerns, and you will also have fun!
- Spend a few days practicing how you will come together to meet:

  Choose one:

  - Play the same song each day that signals students should move to meeting.

  - Use a visual timer that allows two minutes to move.

  - Try call and repeat: Teacher: Good morning, class. Students: Good morning, _____. Teacher: Every day starts with? Students: Community Meeting!

- Explain the four parts of the meeting (times are suggestions):

  - **Check-In** (1–3 minutes) – This is when we check in with classmates and say hello. See resources below for many different ideas.

  - **Group Chat** (4–7 minutes) – This is when we will talk with a partner or the whole group about a topic, how we are feeling, or share news.

  - **Group Activity** (3–5 minutes) – This is a community-building activity that is interactive and fun, and may or may not be academic based.

  - **Daily Agenda** – (2–3 minutes) – Segue into academics. Let the students know what to expect for the day, especially if there are changes in the schedule. Predictability creates safety for many students.

- Resources for running a Monday morning meeting:
  - https://www.panoramaed.com/blog/morning-meeting
  - Morning Meeting Book (Responsive Classroom)
  - https://www.crslearn.org/product/morning-meeting-book/
  - Morning Meeting Character Education Resources (TeachersPayTeachers)
  - https://www.teacherspayteachers.com/Browse/Search:morning%20meeting%20character%20education
  - Morning Meeting Ideas for Middle School (Education World)
  - https://www.educationworld.com/a_admin/admin/admin523.shtml
  - Morning Meeting Pinterest Resources and Freebies

- https://www.pinterest.com/search/pins/?q=morning%20meetings
- Morning Meeting Slides – PowerPoint and Google Slides Versions (TeachersPayTeachers)
- https://www.teacherspayteachers.com/Browse/Search:morning%20meeting%20slides
- What Is Morning Meeting? (Responsive Classroom)
- https://www.responsiveclassroom.org/what-is-morning-meeting/
- Responsive Classroom Morning Meeting Samples (Responsive Classroom)
- https://www.responsiveclassroom.org/sites/default/files/pdf_files/SMMbooklet.pdf

Sample Parent Letter

Dear Parents and Caregivers,

We will begin our school day every morning with a Community Meeting. Our meeting will last 15 to 20 minutes and will include a check-in, group chat, and group activity.

We will meet in a circle and begin by greeting one another by name in a friendly and kind way. Next, students will have a chance to share any new and exciting events with the class or share on a specific topic that I select. This allows them to work on their speaking and listening skills. After sharing, we will do an interactive activity for the whole class. We might sing a song, read a poem, or play a game. This allows the students to work or problem solve as a whole group while learning together.

The last part of our meeting is called Daily Agenda. During this time, students think about the day or week ahead, and reflect on their personal goals. I will let them know what to expect. Our meeting is a great way to build community, increase excitement about learning, and improve academic and social skills for your student.

I look forward to getting to know your student throughout this year. It is always amazing to watch them build friendships and self-confidence during our daily Community Meetings. Please let me know if you have any questions.

Sincerely,

Monday Motivation Meetings (Grades 6–12)

When students enter middle school, the schedule for the day drastically changes from the elementary experience. Students typically change classes many times throughout the day, and the sense of community and belonging can be hard to establish when your group of students changes every hour or hour and a half. The Monday Motivation Meeting was my adaptation of the daily Community Meeting held in elementary school, but adapted to fit a secondary classroom schedule. The meeting is only held on Mondays and is typically 10 minutes. Any time frame from 5 to 15 minutes can work—do what works best for you. The parts are similar in purpose, but the timeframe is shorter.

Community Meeting

CHECK-IN

Group Chat

GROUP ACTIVITY

DAILY AGENDA

15-MINUTE FOCUS
Behavior Interventions Workbook: Your **Roadmap** for Creating a **Positive Classroom Community**

129

Monday Meeting Class Norms

 Respect the speaker.

 Wait your turn and listen.

 What's said here, stays here.

 Words matter.

 Everyone's voice is valuable.

Teacher Directions:

- Inform parents that you will hold a Monday Motivation Meeting each week to build community and start the week with a positive mindset.
- Decide your formation for the meeting (students stay in regular assigned seats or circle up—Stackable stools are a great way to deal with limited space or students can stand in a circle).
- Share your "why" for the weekly meeting with students.
- Ask students to help you generate expectations and norms. (Or use the norms on page 130)

  Explain the four parts of the meeting:
  - **Check In** (1–3 min) – Question of the Day with a partner or hellos.
  - **Group Chat** (3–5 min) – Share a YouTube or TedTalk video with a motivational or inspirational message that introduces a life skill or hot topic.
  - **Community Builder** (3–5 min) – Academic game, fun game, or competition
  - **Agenda** –Share your agenda for the week.

Resources and Activities in Grades 6–12 meetings:

- https://www.youtube.com/watch?v=Mmva9v4AB10&ab_channel=Edutopia
  - Example of secondary school holding school-wide daily community meeting
- https://icebreakerideas.com/icebreakers-high-school-students/
- https://www.signupgenius.com/school/icebreaker-activities-middle-school-high-school.cfm
- https://www.ef.edu/blog/teacherzone/13-fail-safe-icebreakers-use-class-today/

Daily ChitChat

The two previous ideas of hosting structured meetings either daily or once per week for an extended time do not fit in all teachers' schedules or all teaching styles. With that in mind, a daily 3- to 5-minute practice where students have a predictable topic and timeframe to connect with a classmate or whole class offers a community-building opportunity in less time. The Daily ChitChat option is instead of a meeting, not in addition to!

Teacher Directions:

The teacher will set a timer for the allotted time, and students share their response to the theme of the day. They can share in pairs, or the whole class can listen to the few who volunteer. The goal is that everyone will speak or share feedback in some way, so choose the method that works best for your setting.

- Monday Motivation – Share something that has inspired you lately. What keeps you going?
- Tell Me Something Tuesday – Share a story or a funny joke.
- What's Good Wednesday – Share some good news!
- Thankful Thursday – Attitude of Gratitude – Share something you are thankful for.
- Fun Fact Friday – Share random trivia or something about yourself people would not know.

ChitChat

After your teacher sets the timer, share your response to the theme of the day.
You can share in pairs, or the whole class can listen to volunteers. Everyone is invited to participate!

Monday Motivation

Share something that has inspired you lately.
What keeps you going?

Tell Me Something Tuesday

Share a story or a funny joke.

What's Good Wednesday

Share some good news!

Thankful Thursday

Attitude of Gratitude –
Share something you are thankful for.

Fun Fact Friday

Share random trivia or something about yourself
people would not know.

60-Second Closing

Just as we want to start the day or class with a quick check-in, the last few minutes of the day can also be used to not only wrap up content but also serve as time to reflect on successes or challenges. Sixty-second closings build connections and provide students an opportunity to contribute to the group in a low-pressure format. You may choose to have students "circle up" and quickly stand in a circle or as an exit ticket activity using the exit tickets provided.

Teacher Directions:

If students circle up, they are encouraged to share in one or two sentences to keep it moving quickly. I have always allowed students to say "pass" if they do not want to participate, and we just move to the next person. As the year goes on, the number of students who choose to pass decreases.

These closings can be implemented as often as you choose to do them. If the Daily Community Meetings do not work for your setting, these quick closings are a great alternative.

60-Second Closing 1: 3 A's

Ask students to share a moment of appreciation, apology, or an aha!

- Appreciation: something or someone in the class they feel grateful for
- Apology: express an apology to someone or for something
- Aha!: New learning or a moment of understanding that happened as a result of the day's lesson.

60-Second Closing 2: Today/Tomorrow

Ask students to complete this sentence starter:

- Today was _____, and tomorrow will be _____.

60-Second Closing 3: Key Takeaway

Ask students to complete this sentence starter:

- My key takeaway from today is_____.

Helpful Hints:

✓ As the teacher, participate in the activity. This models what you want the students to do and allows them to build connections with you.

✓ Use a visual timer so the students know how much time they have remaining to share.

60-Second Closing Tickets

Appreciation: Today I am grateful for _____.	Today was _____, and tomorrow will be_____.
Apology: Today I would like to apologize to _____ for _____.	My key takeaway today is_____ _____.
Aha!: Today my aha moment came when _____.	Today was _____, and tomorrow will be_____.
Appreciation: Today I am grateful for _____.	My key takeaway today is_____ _____.
Apology: Today I would like to apologize to _____ for _____.	Today was _____, and tomorrow will be_____.
Aha!: Today my aha moment came when _____.	My key takeaway today is_____ _____.
Appreciation: Today I am grateful for _____.	Today was _____, and tomorrow will be_____.
Apology: Today I would like to apologize to _____ for _____.	My key takeaway today is_____ _____.
Aha!: Today my aha moment came when _____.	Today was _____, and tomorrow will be_____.
Appreciation: Today I am grateful for _____.	My key takeaway today is_____ _____.

I Wish My Teacher Knew

A colleague shared a book with me years ago titled, *I Wish My Teacher Knew: How One Question Can Change Everything for Our Kids* by Kyle Schwartz, and it was a game changer. It is such a simple open-ended question, but the information you can learn by asking is remarkable. Some of their responses will be kind, some will be funny, and some will break your heart. As we continue to find ways to build trust with students and let them know we care as much about who they are as we do about their grades, it is little efforts like this that they will appreciate.

Teacher Directions:

- Give every student an index card or use the template on page 136. Ask them to write their name on it.
- Let them know you will not share their cards with any other students.
- Write the question on the board and give them time to respond.
  - It is important to note that if a student shares something that we are obligated to pass on as mandated reporters, we must follow the proper protocols to do so.
- After reading the cards, follow-up with students as needed and time permits.

Sticky Note Campaign

Kiara,

I've noticed how loyal you are to your friends. Keep being a person they can count on.

Mrs. Dean

Of the many strategies I have used over the years, I like to say this one has the greatest return on investment. Writing positive sticky notes only takes a few minutes of your time using a resource you already have, but the impact it has on a student's confidence and the relationship between the two of you is priceless.

It is a simple, yet powerful strategy that many teachers have used to deliver positive feedback to specific students.

Teacher Directions:

- Write down three to five positive characteristics that you want to notice about a student.
- For each positive quality, write two to three sentences on a sticky note.
- The note does not include any suggestions or make any requests for improvement.
- Examples:

  Dear Richard, You are such a creative person! I love hearing your ideas. – Mrs. Dean

  Dear Monique, I appreciate that you always want to help. – Mrs. Dean

On day one, walk past the student's seat and place the note in front of them and keep moving. If the student is not yet a reader, the teacher will stop and read the note. Teachers can also ask the student to read it back to be sure they know what it says. Several days later, a different note is given to the same student. Over two to three weeks, the student will receive all three to five notes.

NOTE: You many want to plan to write notes for two or three students each time you give one to a student in need. This way you can be sure everyone in the class gets one.

I Wish My Teacher Knew Response Cards

I wish my teacher knew…

I wish my teacher knew…

I wish my teacher knew…

I wish my teacher knew…

One-Sentence Intervention

Due to trauma or other life circumstances, some of our students are mistrusting of others, and it can be difficult to connect or build positive relationships with them. They may not trust the "I love ____" messaging of the Sticky Note Campaign, so the One-Sentence Intervention developed by Dr. Jim Fay, author of *Teaching with Love and Logic*, is an excellent alternative. This non-threatening relationship builder helps improve student cooperation and motivation as the teacher lets the student know in a low-key way that they are paying attention.

List six brief statements you can use to notice the student's interests:

Example: "I've noticed you really like to draw."

"I've noticed that _____."

"I've noticed that _____."

"I've noticed that _____."

"I've noticed that _____."

"I've noticed that _____."

"I've noticed that_____."

**Do not end the statement with something like, "…and that's great!"

Helpful Hints:

✓ When and where can you make these statements without embarrassing the child?

✓ Approach the child, smile, and use the statements identified above at least two times a week for at least three weeks.

✓ Do not use this technique when the student is upset. Save it for calm times.

Parking Lot

One of the most common complaints that children have about adults is that we "don't listen" to them. That is obviously true in some instances, but in a classroom setting, it may be that the timing of what the student is trying to ask or share is not working for the adult in that moment. How many times have you said to a student, "Not right now," or "We'll talk about that later," only to forget about it and later becomes never? With the amount of tasks and duties a teacher manages minute to minute, this common oversight can become common practice, and the result is a diminished relationship with the student who is brushed aside.

Having a Parking Lot where students can put their name and know that their teacher will follow up with them builds trust and affirms their thoughts and needs are important.

Teacher Directions:

- Choose a spot in the classroom where students can easily access the Parking Lot poster. Appropriate for ALL grades.

- Hang the poster and provide sticky notes and writing utensils.

- If a student needs to wait to tell you something, ask them to write their name on a note and place it on the Parking Lot Poster. Doing so means the teacher will find the time, find the student, and respond.

- Be consistent! I was good about following up with students, but sometimes it was the next day.

NOTE: I love how this 1st grade teacher divided her Parking Lot into 2 sections – one for "Very Important" and the other for "Fun Stories." Great for younger students who love to tell a random pet story!

Student Satisfaction Survey

As the title of this chapter suggests, "Activities to Use All Year," the Student Satisfaction Survey allows students' voices and opinions to be heard and considered multiple times during the year. This survey is teacher generated and shared only with the teacher. The intent is to gather honest feedback about what is working or not working in the minds of your students. One suggestion: be ready for some tough reading! I allowed my students to give the feedback anonymously because I thought it would be the most valuable, and it was. Just know that kids will be kids and sometimes their brutal honesty can sting.

Teacher Directions:

- Distribute to students every nine weeks or at the end of each semester .

- Allow them to complete it anonymously. (Google form is a great option.)

- Share the consensus in a general way with students. They were always interested.

- Try to make one or two changes based on their feedback. This show of respect and consideration of their opinions goes a long way.

Student Satisfaction Survey

Directions: No name. Please share detailed feedback, *positive* or *negative*. Write as much as necessary and use the back of the paper for more space if needed. Thank you.

Class:_____ Period:_____ Date:_____

What do you like about this class (procedures, set up, teaching methods)? _____

_____

_____

What have been your favorite learning experiences in this class? _____

_____

_____

I don't like it when we _____

_____

_____ .

I wish my teacher would _____

_____

_____ .

When I think of my _____ class, I feel _____

_____

_____ .

I feel I learn best when _____

_____

_____ .

Please list any suggestions you have for _____ class. _____

_____

_____

GROUP ACTIVITIES/GAMES

As the year progresses, student effort and excitement fluctuate between all-in and not-going-to-happen. On occasion, we can add in a few minutes of fun with purpose so students can enjoy their time with one another and their time in your class. The following list includes ideas that are very low-prep for the teacher, but high-energy and fun for students. Sprinkle one in your plans every so often, or if you choose to implement a community meeting, these are great for the group activity!

- **Community People Search**
- **Four Corners**
- **Trading Cards**
- **Same, Same**
- **This or That**

Community People Search

This is a fun, interactive way for students to get to know one another. Each student walks around with the form and a pencil and asks others to sign their paper in the box that states something true about them. Each student may sign only once, and then they must find someone else. It is quick, loud, and full of energy. Have fun!

Four Corners

Four Corners is a community-building activity that can be used in a variety of ways and can easily be incorporated into academic lessons.

Teacher Directions:

Label areas of the room 1 through 4. Laminate the four number signs and post in your room. Explain to the students that four items or statements will be displayed. Students should pick the item that describes them or something they like. When creating your own slides, try to be sure that there is a category for ALL students. I often included three ideas and an "Other" category so every student has a place to stand.

For example, if a student has brown eyes, they will go to area 1 when the slide is displayed. When students arrive at the designated area, they should discuss the posted question. This can be done as many times as the teacher chooses and the activity works well with "getting to know you" as well as with academic discussion questions.

Other ideas:

- Car, Truck, Motorcycle, Other
- Dog, Cat, Fish, Other
- Pizza Hut®, Papa Johns®, Dominos®, Other

Helpful Hints:

✓ Use number labels that are clearly visible to students.

✓ Clearly display discussion topic so students know what to do in the groups.

✓ Have a signal for transition to groups and then for return to their seats.

✓ Use a visual timer or song while in groups so students know how much time is left.

Community People Search

Directions: Walk around the room with this form and a pencil and ask fellow students to sign their name on a line in the box that contains a true statement about them. Each student may sign only one box. Have fun!

I like to make lists.	I care a lot about others' opinions of me.	It drives me crazy when people talk too much.	I am always ready to have some fun.
I like to handle problems on my own.	I get bored very easily.	It is important that others listen to me.	I need friends to accept me for who I am.
It is important to me to be dependable.	I like for everybody to get along.	I like routines and structure.	If I work in a group, I need everybody to do their part.
I struggle with organization.	I like my privacy.	I like to help others with their problems.	I am curious and like to learn new things.
Others would consider me responsible.	I need freedom and variety.	It is important to me to always be kind.	I rarely show my emotions.

Four Corners

1	**Brown Eyes**	
2	**Blue Eyes**	
3	**Green Eyes**	
4	**Other**	

Discussion:

The best thing I did this Summer was…

Trading Cards

This is one of my favorite ways to have students mix and meet with each other to engage in friendly chitchat, discuss an academic concept, or review for an assessment.

Teacher Directions:

- Use a pack of playing cards and distribute one card per student.
- Play music while the students move around and trade cards quickly.
- When the music stops, call out the pairs or groups. Examples: Reds/Blacks, Odds/Evens, Hearts/Clubs, Face Cards/Number Cards
- After 1or 2 minutes, start the music again and yell "Remix!" & students trade again.
- Repeat these steps until you are finished with the topics to discuss.

Same, Same

This is a simple, fun activity with NO materials or prep needed. Let students know they may use **one** of the following three sentences frames:

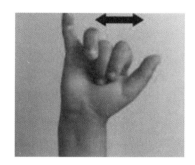

I love _____   I like _____   or   I hate _____

A student shares their one sentence out loud, and all other students who agree with that student either stand and say, "Same, Same" or stay in their seat and say it while using the ASL sign for it. IMPORTANT RULE: No student may put anyone's name in the blank for any of the three choices.

This or That

This is another short, low-prep activity that allows students to quickly see with whom they have various things in common.

(Link to digital presentation: https://docs.google.com/presentation/d/1pt3H8LhTeZGXPQk58K_iqCt4RuegDrdueZWM0lpyPNA/edit?usp=sharing)

Teacher Directions:

Explain to students that they will see two images on each slide and to indicate which item they prefer by following directions. Your directions for student agreement can vary based on age of students, time, and space available for movement.

Agreement Examples:

- If you prefer image 1, stand up

- If you prefer image 2, stay seated

- If you prefer image 1, raise your hand

- If you prefer image 2, touch your nose

- If you prefer image 1, walk to the left wall

- If you prefer image 2, walk to the right wall

- If you prefer image 1, type 1 in the chat

- If you prefer image 2, type 2 in the chat

Keeping Your Community Strong–
Activities to Use All Year
Chapter 5 Roadmap (Planning Guide)

Activity Choose 1 or 2 to try after the first few weeks.	Action Items: What do you need to complete?	Date: When do you plan to use?	Page #
COMMUNITY BUILDERS			
Daily Community Meetings (Gr K-5)			
Monday Motivation Meetings (Gr 6-12)			
Daily ChitChat			
60-Second Closing – 3 Options			
I Wish My Teacher Knew			
Sticky Note Campaign			
One-Sentence Intervention			
Parking Lot			
Student Satisfaction Survey			
GROUP ACTIVITIES/GAMES			
Community People Search			
Four Corners			
Trading Cards			
Same, Same			
This or That			

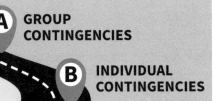

CHAPTER SIX

Classroom Contingencies, Group Goals, and Celebrations

Ⓐ **GROUP CONTINGENCIES**

Ⓑ **INDIVIDUAL CONTINGENCIES**

Alone we can do so little; together we can do so much. – Helen Keller

There are many articles, books, research studies, and opinions about using incentives with students to promote positive behavior. This entire workbook could be dedicated to the meta-analysis of it, and it still wouldn't touch what has been said, proven, or disproven. I have personally read about or been trained on at least ten different approaches on behavior management, and I imagine many educators would align with this experience. What I have learned is that you can find research to support any side of anything. Now, obviously that is a bit of an exaggeration, but it often seems to be true in the world of education.

One of the ways I reconcile these ideas of "earning for effort" in the classroom setting is this: we are preparing students to become professionals. In many professions, meeting and exceeding your goals affords you privileges and opportunities. Therefore, in this classroom, when you work hard, persevere, and meet or exceed your goals, there will be occasional chances for you to earn privileges and opportunities. Many organizations, sports teams, and corporations have various recognition programs and bonus earning opportunities for their athletes and employees. In the classroom, it has not mattered to me if students were working hard because the grade was important to them or because they were excited about an earning opportunity. I was just happy they were working hard.

I say all of that to make this point: in my thirty years working with students, I have found that both intrinsic and extrinsic motivation have a time and place in the classroom. Of course, we want students of all ages to walk into school each day excited and ready to learn, to follow directions when given, and to only attend to the tasks we assign. But if you have spent more than ten minutes in a classroom of humans, you know it is rare to have everyone in the same place academically or emotionally for extended periods of time. For these reasons and several more, I have used extrinsic motivators every year with every group of students and have found great success. Plainly said, it works.

Section One of this chapter focuses on group contingencies, which have been cited as highly effective in the research because "contingency programs are often the best way to reduce problematic behaviors, reinforce good behaviors, and teach important skills. Group contingencies—behavior management programs that provide reinforcements and rewards for more than one person—save time and resources and encourage members of the group to cooperate with one another."[8]

 GROUP CONTINGENCIES

Types of Group Contingencies

There are three types of group contingencies: dependent, independent, and interdependent.
A dependent group contingency offers a reward to an entire group based upon the behavior or performance

of one or more of the group's members. I like to call this the "hero" strategy. One or two students have a specific goal on which they are focusing, and when the student meets the goal the entire group or class earns an incentive because of the individual's efforts. When this approach is used, the classmates are typically invested in the hero student meeting their goals, so encouragement and support are given. Positive energy is also given when everyone gets to celebrate.

The independent group contingency provides incentives to the members of the group who meet a specific goal, but only the members of the group who meet the goal get to participate in any extrinsic incentive. Some educators see the advantage of this type of contingency plan in that it holds each student accountable for meeting the goal individually, and students who did not meet the goal are not rewarded without earning it.

The last type, interdependent contingencies, only allow an incentive to be earned if all members of the group meet the specific goal. If one student does not meet the criteria, then nobody in the group earns. I have not used this approach exactly as it is defined, but I have used it successfully with slight modifications so specific students are not held solely responsible for a loss in the eyes of their peers.

Each of these types has value in certain situations when managed well. I encourage you to read through the options and find what best fits your classroom culture, the needs of your students, and the expectations of your administration. Most importantly, I recommend choosing the idea to which you will be the most dedicated and consistent in implementing as this will greatly dictate the success or failure of any approach.

Group Contingencies

The following ideas are shared as options. They are similar in their approaches and desired outcomes, but each one has its own twist, and I am confident that you will find one that fits your needs. Teachers should only use one at a time, but you may find the need to change things as the year progresses, so you can revisit the list or adapt to make it feel fresh to your students. I have used or seen all of these in various classrooms K–12. What you call it and how you introduce it will impact student buy-in, so student age is a consideration, but not an absolute factor.

My Time/Your Time

MY TIME	YOUR TIME
III	⊪⊪ ⊪⊪

There are two ways to manage this strategy:

1. Daily: Predetermine how many minutes you can spare at the end of the class/day (up to five minutes). Put that number of tally marks on the board at the beginning of class. Tell the class, "Each time I lose a minute of 'my' teaching time due to disruptions, the class will lose a minute of 'your' time." The teacher erases a point under "your time" and writes it in under "my time." The five minutes at the end of class could be talk time, homework time, choice time, etc.

2. Weekly: The second option is to start with no marks on the chart. When the class meets a goal (no disruptions for 10 minutes, all students seated for 10 minutes, etc.) the class earns a point under "your time." If they do not meet the goal or have a large disruption, the teacher earns a point under "my time." All points add up throughout the week and the difference between your time/my time points equals the number of minutes of preferred activity for the class on Friday. (See the chart on the previous page. The class earned seven minutes of preferred activity on Friday because they beat the teacher 10-3 Monday – Thursday.)

Helpful Hints:

✓ Introduce the system to the students and allow questions and input.

✓ Students should generate reasons why the teacher will earn a point as well as different ways to use their minutes when they earn them.

✓ In the first few days of using this, stop and explain why you are moving a point to the teacher's side of the chart. Let them ask questions and remind them of the expectations.

✓ Continue to vary the privileges earned to hold interest.

Success Chain

This has been one of my personal favorites because students loved it, and I was able to make many adjustments to it to fit a specific group's needs.

Teacher Directions:

• Establish the Behavior to Work On for the class. This could be number of verbal disruptions, out-of-seat behaviors, or any other area the class could improve.

• Choose a space on the whiteboard that can be dedicated to the Behavior to Work On. Write the number of points as tally marks that they will start with each day. My suggestions are as follows:

    - If you are having 10-15 disruptions per hour – start with five marks.
    - 15-20 disruptions per hour – start with eight marks.
    - More than 20 – start with 10 marks.
    - The marks start over each day.

• Explain to the class that they are being given _____number of chances to start each day. Each time there is an infraction (Behavior to Work On) one mark is erased. As long as they have ONE mark left at the end of the designated time, a link on the chain is earned.

• You may choose to offer opportunities to earn "special" links for meeting specific goals.

    - Hallway Link – excellent transition in the hallway
    - Visitor's Link – met expectations when a visitor entered the room
    - MVP Link – One student met a personal behavior goal – write student name on the link
    - Compliment Link – class earned a compliment from another staff member
    - Extra Mile Link – multiple students giving extra efforts in some way
    - Academic Efforts – set an academic goal for the class to achieve

• Once the chain has _____ number of links, they earn a class-wide privilege.

Helpful Hints:

✓ Survey the students in advance for class-wide privilege ideas. Select three to five from their list that you are willing and able to do.

✓ Let them know at the beginning of each round what they are working toward.

✓ 10 to win is a good start. 10 links = earned privilege. Next round is 12 links, then 14 links, etc. For some classes, the goal was only five links.

✓ If one or two students constantly lose points for the class, cease erasing points for their behavior. They can use an individual system (found in Chapter 7) to work on personal goals. If they achieve the individual goals, they can participate in the class privilege. If not, ask a team member if the student can participate in their class during the privilege.

Table Pennies with VIP Table

This strategy is intended for K–2nd grades. Each table group has a small bucket in the center of the table. If the students are in desks, place the buckets together in a location in the front of the room with numbers for the groups.

Teacher Directions:

- Generate a list of ways that the table groups can earn pennies.
- Post the list in words/pictures.
- Use plastic or real pennies and keep them in a bucket or something easily accessible.
- Drop pennies in buckets when expectations are being met. They love the penny drops!
- It is acceptable to give pennies only to groups who meet expectations.
- Once earned, pennies cannot be lost.
- Each group gets to count their pennies at the end of the day and color in their total on the Penny Poster.
- On Fridays, students purchase privileges with their pennies from the Penny Store. Use coupons for this so there is no cost to the teacher.
- The table with the most pennies is the VIP table for the week and gets a plastic tablecloth with a dollar tree centerpiece and the class stuffed animal for the day (or something else you come up with)!
- If a student needs their own bucket and it works better with them as a lone ranger, do it. It is a win for everyone.

Penny Poster

Group Name(s): _____ Week of: _____

Penny Store

Awesome Sticker
5 pennies/5¢

Use a Fancy Pencil or Pen
10 pennies/10¢

Coupon Caddy Visit
15 pennies/15¢

No Homework
20 pennies/20¢

Sit with a Friend in Class
25 pennies/25¢

Free Computer Time
30 pennies/30¢

Lunch with a Friend
35 pennies/35¢

Secret Bonus
40 pennies/40¢

Class Wallet

This strategy can be used for any grade! I suggest using the dry erase page protectors, which can be found anywhere office supplies are sold. Mine came from Dollar Tree®. I have used Monopoly® money in the past, but I have included some Class Cash you can use for this strategy or in any way it fits your classroom goals.

Teacher Directions:

- Write the class goal and privilege on the top of the page protector.
- (Ex.: $20 = 15 minutes tech time, 15 min extra recess, or 15 min of class games)
- Establish the criteria for earning class cash. Post the criteria.
- When earned, place the cash in the class wallet so all students can see it. Multiple earning opportunities per day is encouraged, but at least one per day.
- If you teach multiple classes, add a name to the top of each one or use different colors.
- Use $1 bills unless something amazing happens in which they can earn the very rare larger bill.
- Once earned, the cash cannot be lost. It is possible not to earn cash in a day if criteria are not met.
- Individual students who purposely try to prevent the group from earning can have their own goal or wallet so as not to sabotage the group.

VIP Student

The VIP student, or Very Improved Person, is a great way to recognize any individual who has improved in any way. I love this because it allows our students who really struggle with behavior or academics to have an opportunity to be recognized and celebrated even for minimal improvement. Any step in the right direction is a good one!

Teacher Directions:

- Choose one or more students each Friday or Monday as a VIP for the day.
- The student must have shown improvement in some way during the week.
- The student is announced first thing in the morning and receives a VIP certificate, a VIP badge for special privileges, and a VIP desk sign if that works for your setting.
- The VIP badge allows student access to the VIP supply bucket, favorite seating areas, water and restroom privileges throughout the day, and any other fun ideas you generate.
- Print a certificate for the student to take home.
- Print and laminate the VIP badges, hole punch, and put on lanyards for elementary students.
- Print the VIP table signs and frame in 4x6 frame to sit at student's seat for the day.

congratulations!

You have reached VIP status!

_____
STUDENT

Thank you so much for your hard work and dedication in this class.

Your effort to improve

is appreciated and has earned you VIP Status for the day.

I am very proud of you! Keep up the good work!

_____
TEACHER

VIP
VERY IMPROVED PERSON

Congratulations!

You have reached VIP status!

_____
STUDENT

Thank you so much for your
hard work and dedication in this class.

Your effort to improve

_____

is appreciated and has earned you
VIP Status for the day.

I am very proud of you! Keep up the good work!

_____
TEACHER

Congratulations!

You have reached VIP status!

_____
STUDENT

Thank you so much for your
hard work and dedication in this class.

Your effort to improve

_____

is appreciated and has earned you
VIP Status for the day.

I am very proud of you! Keep up the good work!

_____
TEACHER

Exclusive Permission
to Special Privileges
in the Classroom

Exclusive Permission
to Special Privileges
in the Classroom

Exclusive Permission
to Special Privileges
in the Classroom

Exclusive Permission
to Special Privileges
in the Classroom

Mount in a 4" x 6" frame and place on VIP student's desk.

Golden Ticket

Another option for student recognition or group/class recognition is any version of the Golden Ticket. The Golden Ticket affords the owner/group special privileges they have earned with their efforts or achievement. One example that truly inspired me is that of Urban Prep Academy in Chicago. This charter high school for young men requires students to wear uniforms daily, and part of that uniform is a red tie. When a student is nominated by a classmate or staff member for doing something exceptional, they are given a gold tie to wear for the week so all students and staff will recognize their achievement. They also receive a red and gold striped tie when they are accepted to a four-year college. (Read about the ties here: https://www.tiemart. com/blogs/tiepedia/customer-spotlight-urban-prep-academies. You can also watch an awesome video detailing this ritual at https://www.youtube.com/watch?v=Mmva9v4AB10.)

Most public schools do not wear uniforms, so the gold tie ceremony/ritual may not fit your setting, but there are many variations of this that could be considered. Anything that could be spray-painted gold can work (Golden Plate, Golden Cup, Golden Mascot, Golden Calculator, Golden Paw, etc.)!

Share criteria for earning the "Golden Cup" with students and create a way for students to see their progress toward earning it. This is the one strategy that I would suggest having middle or high school classes compete to earn. This would be in addition to another point system as a bonus opportunity. If you use Class Wallet, you could have the "Golden Hundo" or "Golden Benjamin" that could take the class to the next level of privileges very quickly.

MVP Card

This is an example of a "hero" strategy. The MVP is a dependent contingency to be used in conjunction with any of the whole group systems listed above. The purpose of the MVP card is to help reduce the frequency of specific behaviors from an individual student.

Teacher Directions:

- I suggest using either a 5, 10, 15, or 20-minute interval to start. I have used three minutes on a few occasions.
- Collect baseline data on the frequency of the behavior to work on in order to decide the starting interval time.
- If a five-minute interval is chosen, each box represents five minutes.
- If possible, the student will have the timer on their desk, and they should set and reset it independently.
- If at the end of the specified time, the student has not disrupted, the student can check/color one box.
- When each box has a check mark, a privilege is earned for the *whole class*.
- The boxes do not have to be checked consecutively.
- After a student has achieved a card two times at the same time interval, the time should be increased. (Ex: (2) five-minute cards achieved, student will now receive a 10-minute card to start.)
- Use www.wheelofnames.com or an app such as Wheel Decide to create an MVP wheel of privileges. These should be quick – three minutes of talk time, three minutes of recess, three minutes of tech, etc. When the MVP achieves, the outcome for all should be quick and free for the teacher.

MVP Card

NAME	TARGET BEHAVIOR	

MVP Card

NAME	TARGET BEHAVIOR	

MVP Card

NAME	TARGET BEHAVIOR	

Behavior Tracking Apps Available

Most educators are familiar with ClassDojo or PBIS Rewards, but I wanted to provide a list of several more that are out there worth checking out. My personal favorite is Live School because of the individual and House Points, built-in rewards store, as well as a paycheck with student data that can be printed or shared. Each of these on this list brings something unique and valuable to behavior tracking and management. This chart does not include all that are out there, but these are the ones I have experienced or observed in a classroom.

Name	Website	Free/Paid	Grade Level Suggestions	iOS/Android
Bloomz	https://www.bloomz.com/	Paid	PreK–8	iOS and Android
ClassCharts	https://www.classcharts.com	Paid	K–4	Web-based
Classcraft	https://www.classcraft.com	Paid	3–12	iOS and Android
ClassDojo	https://www.classdojo.com	Free	PreK–8	iOS and Android
Classroom Carrots	https://www.carrotrewards.co.uk	Paid	K–8	iOS and Android
KidConnect Classroom App	https://www.teachemotionalregulation.com	Free for 1 Student/Paid	K–5	iOS (iPad only)
Live School	https://www.whyliveschool.com	Paid	K–12	Web-based
PBIS Reward	https://www.pbisrewards.com	Paid	K–12	iOS and Android

Tools to Support Positive Systems

Pick Your Privileges

Students love the variety that randomizer websites allow teachers to create. Check out the following to create your own custom wheels that students will spin to see what they have earned when they have achieved a goal.

- www.wheelofnames.com – FREE & all wheels can be saved and used endlessly with a free account.
- www.wheeldecide.com
- www.randomlists.com
- www.randomnamepicker.net

Teacher Directions:

- Set a goal and ALL students must achieve. (Ex.: all arrived on time, completed homework, earned at least a certain grade on a quiz, no one interrupted the speaker, etc.)
- Keep a record of when goals are met.
- Chart the data and use it to discuss what needs improvement.
- Predetermine the goal and when goal is met, someone gets to spin the wheel and everyone receives the privilege.

Classroom Coupons and Coupon Caddy

Teachers have been spending their own time and money filling up treasure boxes, snack stashes, school supply drawers, and much more for years. I have recommended moving away from these money pits because although they are fun, $20 here and there all year long adds up. Of course, if any educator is willing and able to fund such things, go ahead! We know they can be fun and exciting. You may also want to consider options that are very low cost to completely free—and still fun! My go-to for finding coupons is www.teacherspayteachers.com (search for *classroom reward coupons*). Once the list of thousands pops up, filter by free to see hundreds of options. Spend a little time looking for coupons that fit your setting and the age of your students, and print away.

Photo Credit: https://proudtobeprimary.com/classroom-management-coupons-for-kids/. Check out proudtobeprimary.com for awesome freebies and ideas!

I love how this educator has created a "Coupon Caddy" to keep the privileges organized and easy for student shopping. This idea can be used for ALL grades K-12. The coupons just need to contain privileges or opportunities that appeal to the age of your students. One thing I know for sure – people never age out of wanting to be a winner!

Scratch-Off Tickets

Check out these fun, silver scratch-off labels. These range from $7 and up for 100 or more labels on Amazon and Etsy. Use these to stick over the reward listed on your classroom coupons. Students love the mystery of the scratch-off! They choose this coupon from the caddy and use a coin to scratch and find their privilege earned.

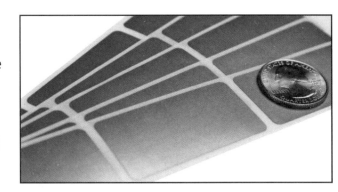

NOTE: Please remember you want to choose one of the whole group strategies and then possibly use an individual strategy on an as-needed basis. Students want to be successful, and they want to be recognized for their efforts. Help them by noticing them when they work hard, achieve goals, and meet expectations. If we are going to notice our students when they are wrong, why not notice them when they are right? Stay positive and do what works for you.

Classroom Contingencies, Group Goals, and Celebrations

Chapter 6 Roadmap (Planning Guide)

Activity Choose 1 from each section	Action Items: What do you need to complete?	Date: When do you plan to use?	Page #
GROUP CONTINGENCIES			
My Time/Your Time			
Success Chain			
Table Pennies with VIP Table			
Class Wallet/Class Cash			
INDIVIDUAL CONTINGENCIES			
VIP Student Kit (Four pages)			
Golden Ticket			
MVP Card			
Behavior Tracking Apps			
Pick Your Privileges – Random Wheel Sites			
Classroom Coupons and Coupon Caddy			
Scratch-Off Tickets			

De-Escalation, Behavior Support, and Behavior Problem-Solving

A DE-ESCALATION/LANGUAGE OF DISAGREEMENT

B BEHAVIOR PROBLEM-SOLVING

C BEHAVIOR SUPPORT TOOLS

You can't teach children to behave better by making them feel worse. When children feel better, they behave better. – Pam Leo

Setting high expectations for student behavior and communicating those expectations clearly is key for maintaining a positive classroom community. High expectations also show respect for, and confidence in, our students' abilities to achieve. In addition to holding students accountable to these expectations, it is important to provide support and compassion when they struggle to meet them. This is an area where there is room for growth for most of us. The high expectations are there, but the teacher may not know how to (or be willing to) provide the necessary support when students fall short. Even when we want to be supportive, the behavior challenges have been a source of frustration; have led to a loss of instructional minutes; and have negatively impacted relationships, making daily resets difficult. It's easy to see why offering support for challenging behavior is a challenge in itself!

The powerful quote from Dr. Ross Greene, "Kids do well if they can," reminds us to look at behavior as a problem to solve rather than a person to fix. If you have a student who is not doing well, it is rarely because they do not *want* to do well. Often, there is a barrier that they are struggling to overcome. When students feel connected, capable, calm, *and* supported, we will see positive changes in their behavior. When emotional needs are ignored or trivialized, students' feelings of anger, frustration, hurt, or resistance may result in behaviors that can destroy our classroom community.

There are few things that I am more passionate about than helping challenging students improve their self-confidence and strengthen their belief that they can make positive changes. Students who struggle with behavior and self-regulation have been a part of my every day for thirty years, and I have invested thousands of hours learning about and implementing interventions that have worked for both students and teachers. This chapter is designed to help streamline the process of finding solutions for the most common behavior challenges in K–12 classrooms. Support for hard-to-reach students is not always easy to give or easy for students to accept. They may need to see you in action for a while before they trust your intentions and are willing to take the risk of letting you in. I encourage you to stick with it. A student's hesitation is rarely personal. They want and need your support, and every effort you make matters.

NOTE: The ideas in this chapter do not replace a full Functional Behavioral Assessment (FBA) or development of a Behavior Intervention Plan. Instead, these ideas provide various strategies and planning tools to employ before deciding that an FBA is necessary. Consulting with the professionals in your building or district who are highly skilled or trained in behavior support may also guide you in your decision making.

De-Escalation: How & Why

"Emotions are the gateway to student's learning. When content is introduced, in only a split second, a student's emotions decide if they are interested or not. The brain hasn't even had a chance to consider the information rationally before it has been accepted or rejected by the emotions. *Emotions drive attention and attention drives learning, memory, problem solving, and just about everything else.*" – Dr. Robert Sylwester[9]

> "Happy, calm children learn best."
> —Daniel Goleman

In most instances when a student shows disrespectful or explosive behavior, it is preceded by an emotion. The student's inability to cope with or regulate their emotions results in negative behavior, which leads to negative adult reactions and punitive consequences. Fortunately, self-regulation, or the ability to control one's emotions, thoughts, and behaviors, is a skill that can be taught and learned. If we teach specific coping skills prior to stressful events, in addition to using de-escalation techniques during stressful events, we can minimize the most aggressive and explosive behaviors.

De-escalation techniques are often difficult to implement because they go against our natural fight-or-flight reflexes. Remaining calm and professionally detached is not natural and therefore is a skill that needs to be practiced. If we focus on our goals instead of our feelings in the most difficult moments, we are more likely to be a catalyst for calm instead of chaos. We want to:

RESPOND vs. REACT

Adults often try to lecture and correct when student behavior is escalating. Our goal should be to *reduce the level of agitation* and help the student move from survival brain to learning brain. Once that occurs, the student and teacher are more likely to engage in productive discussion.

We have all seen that teacher or staff member who excels in the art of de-escalation with students—maybe you are one of those educators. What are the common behaviors among the people we have identified as masters of this skill?

Adult Behaviors that Help to De-Escalate an Event

- Speak calmly and quietly
- Speak respectfully (privately, if possible)
- Avoid power struggles—use "I" statements
- Allow student time and space to respond
- Acknowledge and praise even minimal cooperation
- Keep your distance; move slowly
- Minimize "power" body language—instead have calm hands/neutral stance
- Position body to the side of student and/or get to eye level
- Keep words brief; stay on agenda

I like to remember it this way: BREATHE.

BREATHE – Steps for *adults* to take when helping a student find calm.

Be Calm. Be the adult. – Somebody has to be!

Respectful tone. – Use it even when they don't "deserve" it.

Eyes or Ears. – Allow students to *listen* if holding eye contact is an issue.

ASK questions. – Would you like to try again? What do you need? Please tell me—I want to help.

Take time to listen and keep your words minimal.

Help when you can. – Their behavior is their way of asking for your help.

Expect the BEST. – They sense it either way.

Maybe you will find it helpful to hang the BREATHE plan where you can see it to help in those truly tough moments when your emotions are telling you to do the opposite of these steps. I have been there as a teacher and as a mom. Trying to de-escalate a child when you are also escalated is like riding a bike with no hands! It is a struggle with a lot of flailing. If you can focus on what your end-goal is, rather than how you feel in the moment, you will be more likely to find success.

De-Escalation - Prevention Strategies

Coaching Language vs. Catching Language

The words we choose when student behavior starts to decline often causes unintended power struggles with students who are oppositional. If you have students in your classroom who question everything or test limits, consider using these phrases to reduce power struggles and increase cooperation. Stating directions in positive terms (saying what you want students to do instead of what not to do) is an effective approach to minimize defiance because it reduces the opportunity for argument.

Try This – Coaching Language	Instead of This – Catching Language
I'll begin when everyone is seated.	Sit down! We are starting now.
We can talk when your voice sounds like mine.	Don't use that tone with me!
Papers turned in on time will receive full credit.	Turn your paper in on time or you will lose points.
Those that are following the rules of the game may continue playing.	Stop breaking the rules of the game.
Please use your words so I can understand what you need.	Stop screaming!
I can help those who are seated.	Don't run around my classroom.
I will be happy to discuss this when the arguing stops.	Stop arguing with me.
Feel free to return when you are calm.	Don't come back to my classroom until you have learned to show respect.
Those who arrive on time will leave on time.	Don't be late to class.

Language of Disagreement

Most adults have experienced a behavioral incident with a student that started as a minor infraction but quickly escalated to a major one because of tone of voice, volume, and word selection. There are several reasons this is such a common issue in adult/child or teacher/student relationships. Analyze a few questions for yourself first:

- Where did you learn how to be respectful as a child?
- How did you learn the expectations or rules of respect in your environment?
- Do you believe your students have been taught the same rules and expectations in their home environments?

If you answered "no" to the last question, it's important to consider:

***Should they know how to respect you according to your practice of respect
if it does not align with their families' practices?***

There are many different meanings and possible interpretations when an adult says to a student, "You are being disrespectful." Since "disrespectful" means different things to different people, educators should provide specific examples of disrespectful behavior and examples of what students should do instead. Offering alternative options, and time to practice, make mistakes, and recover, is an example of coaching students rather than catching students.

Teacher Directions:

- **TEACH the Language of Disagreement** – This involves teaching students how to communicate when they are angry or frustrated, *prior* to them feeling that way. If you teach them in advance, you can use a prompt or gentle reminder when behavior is triggered or escalating. Try saying, "Four words, please," or "Try that with I, please."
- **Practice and Post** the language (see the two example posters) you want them to use when they do get angry or frustrated. Use agreed-upon prompts to remind them of what you've practiced or point to the anchor chart in the room. "Try with I," or "four words, please."
- **Ask the right kind of questions** that lead students to self-correct.
  - Would you like to try that again?
  - Can you think of a different way to say that?
  - Do you want to take a minute before we talk?
  - I am happy to listen when your voice is a Level One.
  - Can I help you figure this out?
  - Is everything okay?
  - What do you need? Please tell me so I can see if I can help.

Four-Word Strategy

A common source of conflict in both classroom and non-classroom environments is direct and blatant defiance of adult requests. I have polled thousands of teachers, asking them to identify student behaviors that were their "hot button" non-negotiables, and being told "no" has always been in the top two.

The Four-Word Strategy is simple: "Yes ma'am, may I… or Yes sir, may I?" It is very important to note that we should offer alternatives to students who are not comfortable with "ma'am" and "sir." This is a response that is considered respectful to some and not to others, so I offer the following options as you can see on the Four-Word Poster:

Yes ma'am/sir, may I…

Yes, may I…

Sure, may I…

I heard you, may I…

Okay, may I

If a student does not want to do what the adult has asked, rather than saying no, they are allowed to use the Four-Word Strategy to preface a request to do something other than what they've been asked. This strategy gives students the language to request permission rather than defy, when they want to do something differently. I understand many adults will take issue with this idea because they believe student compliance equals respect. This strategy is for those students who struggle with compliance and can dominate a classroom with their negative behavior choices and lack of respect for authority. It has been a very effective alternative to power struggles and behavior escalation.

Affective or "I" Statements

Affective statements are an important part of verbal de-escalation. When a person feels they are being blamed, it's common that they respond with defensive behaviors such as arguing, yelling, or threatening. Affective statements, or "I" statements, are a simple way of speaking to students that can help avoid this trap by reducing feelings of blame and focusing on solving a problem. A good "I" statement takes responsibility for one's own feelings, while also *describing* the problem. Rather than telling a student what they are, you are telling them how their behavior is affecting you, which teaches empathy and self-awareness while also using de-escalating language. Win-win.

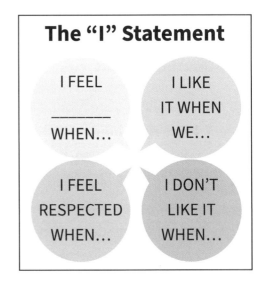

The "I" Statement

I FEEL _____ WHEN…

I LIKE IT WHEN WE…

I FEEL RESPECTED WHEN…

I DON'T LIKE IT WHEN…

Sample Affective Statement Sentence Starters:

- I don't like it when…
- I feel _____ when…
- I like it when we…
- I feel respected when…
- I feel disrespected when…

The Language of Disagreement

Four-Word Strategy

Choose from:

Yes ma'am/sir

Yes, Sure, Absolutely, I hear you.

+ May I?

The Language of Disagreement

Try with "I" Statements

I don't like it when...

I need you to...

I feel _____ when...

I like it when...

I am asking for...

I Feel Reflection Form

I feel _____

when _____

because _____ .

I would like _____ .

I feel _____

when _____

because _____ .

I would like _____ .

Decision Makers Basket

(Credit: Shawna Griffin)

This strategy is designed to reduce tattling, peer conflict, and help students become problem solvers that are comfortable managing their own conflicts.

When students are in groups or working together for projects, place a basket in the center of the table or in an area where students can access it. In each basket, place the following items:

- Dice (I prefer large foam ones)
- A coin (I prefer oversized plastic ones)
- A deck of cards
- Slips of blank paper

Encourage students to use decision-making strategies before engaging in arguments or tattling.

- **Odd or Even**: One person is odd; the other is even. Roll a die; if the number displayed is odd then that person gets to share their idea first or "wins" the argument.
- **High or Low**: Each person draws a card and the person with the highest card gets to make the decision.
- **Heads or Tails**: Use the coins to play heads or tails to decide who gets to go first.
- **Team Decision:** The students use the blank slips of paper to vote for the idea or decision they want to win.
- **Rock, Paper, Scissors** is another great tool for choosing who gets to go first or make the decision.

Breathing Exercises

One of the obvious signs that a student is upset or agitated is shallow or short breathing. It is typically not helpful to use the words "calm down" with an agitated or angry student, but it may be helpful to remind them of a breathing strategy that will help them feel calmer. These strategies must be introduced prior to an event when emotions are escalated. When we are calm, our body is in what is known as "rest and digest" mode, or learning brain. When our breathing is normal, our muscles are relaxed, and heart rate is in the normal range. For students, it may look like reading a book, watching a video, or talking to friends and relaxing. There are many apps, videos, and websites to choose from to learn specific breathing techniques that are proven to help calm the nervous system, thus creating a calm mental state. These are a few favorite breathing exercises:

- **STAR Breathing** – Use the STAR breathing photo in a calming space, calm down kit, or on a student's desk. Start breathing in and trace the star to the count of five on each point. Student breathes in, holds for five, breathes out, and repeats until the star has been traced.
- **Pinwheel Breathing** – Teacher can include a pinwheel as a calming tool in the classroom or teach students how to use their own fingers to do it. Take your two pointer fingers and point them toward each other in front of your mouth. Circle one finger over the other while inhaling and exhaling, blowing on the fingers to make a noise like a pinwheel.
- **Square Breathing** – The student can use a photo of a square or draw an imaginary square while breathing in for two sides and exhaling for two sides. Repeat four to five times.
- **Volcano Breathing** – Student should press hands together in a palm-to-palm position with elbows out. Press hard as you breathe in and hands slowly go up over the head like lava through a volcano, then exhale loudly as the hands (lava) go up and over and come back to pressed-hand position to repeat.

Decision-Makers

Attach these instructions to the Decision-Makers Basket

Odd or Even:

One person is odd; the other is even. Roll a die; if the number displayed is odd then that person gets to share their idea first or "wins" the argument.

High or Low:

Each person draws a card and the person with the highest card gets to make the decision.

Heads or Tails:

Use the coins to play heads or tails to decide who gets to go first.

Team Decision:

The students use the blank slips of paper to vote for the idea or decision they want to win.

Rock, Paper, Scissors:

This is another great tool for choosing who gets to go first or make the decision.

Odd or Even:

One person is odd; the other is even. Roll a die; if the number displayed is odd then that person gets to share their idea first or "wins" the argument.

High or Low:

Each person draws a card and the person with the highest card gets to make the decision.

Heads or Tails:

Use the coins to play heads or tails to decide who gets to go first.

Team Decision:

The students use the blank slips of paper to vote for the idea or decision they want to win.

Rock, Paper, Scissors:

This is another great tool for choosing who gets to go first or make the decision.

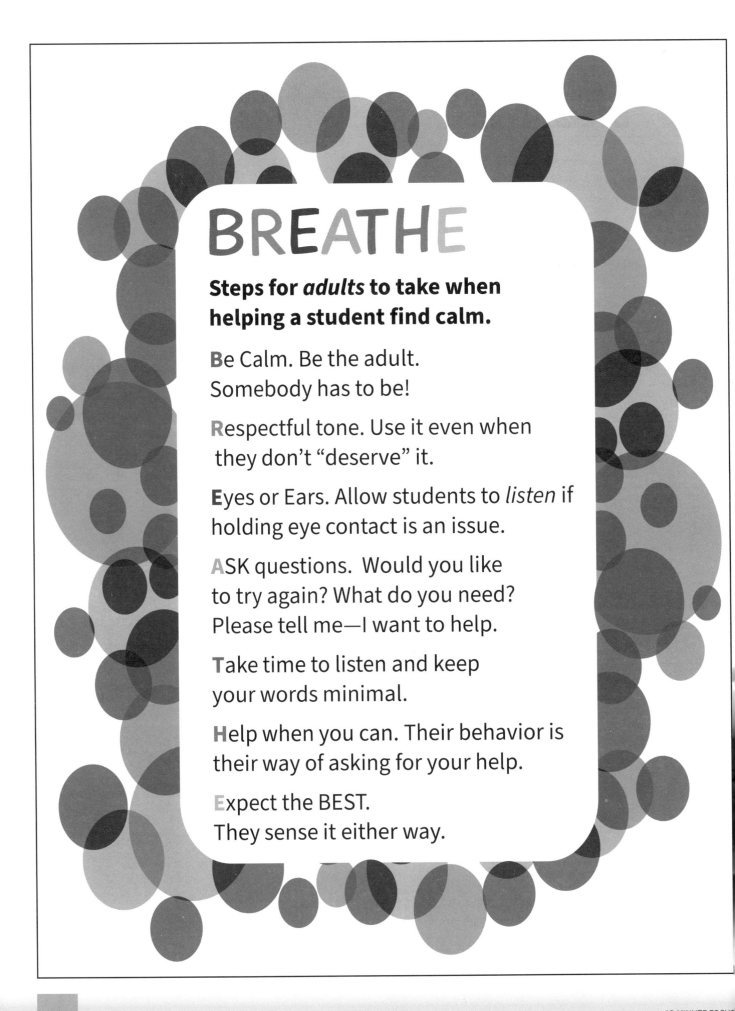

BREATHE

Steps for *adults* to take when helping a student find calm.

Be Calm. Be the adult. Somebody has to be!

Respectful tone. Use it even when they don't "deserve" it.

Eyes or Ears. Allow students to *listen* if holding eye contact is an issue.

ASK questions. Would you like to try again? What do you need? Please tell me—I want to help.

Take time to listen and keep your words minimal.

Help when you can. Their behavior is their way of asking for your help.

Expect the BEST. They sense it either way.

STAR
Breathing

Breathe in
for a count of five.

Breathe out
for a count of five.

STAR
Breathing

Breathe in
for a count of five.

Breathe out
for a count of five.

STAR
Breathing

Breathe in
for a count of five.

Breathe out
for a count of five.

STAR
Breathing

Breathe in
for a count of five.

Breathe out
for a count of five.

Calming Apps & YouTube Resources

Name	Website	Free/Paid	Grade Levels	iOS/Android
BetterSleep: Relax and Sleep	www.bettersleep.com	Free	All ages	iOS and Android
Breathe, Think, Do with Sesame	www.sesamestreetincommunities.org	Free	Ages 2–5	iOS and Android
Calm	www.calm.com	Free	All ages	iOS and Android
Calm Counter Social Story & Anger Management Tool	www.touchautism.com	Paid	Ages 3–12	iOS
Chill Outz	www.chilloutz.com	Paid	Ages 3–8	iOS and Android
DreamyKid Meditation App	www.dreamykid.com	Free	All ages	iOS and web access
emotionary by Funny Feelings	www.emotionary.ai	Free	Ages 4+	iOS
Headspace	www.headspace.com	Free	All ages	iOS and Android
Positive Penguins		Paid	Ages 4–10	iOS and Android
Super Stretch Yoga	www.adventuresofsuperstretch.com	Free	Ages 3–10	iOS
Smiling Mind	www.smilingmind.com.au	Free	Ages 7–18	iOS and Android

34 YouTube videos all linked on one page! This site includes videos for meditation, yoga, positive affirmations, and fun calming techniques. There is something for all ages: https://educationtothecore.com/2020/12/youtube-videos-that-teach-calming-techniques-for-kids/

Code Word

This is a very simple strategy that allows an agreed-upon code word between adult and student to be used as a verbal prompt for a specific behavior. It may be code for sit down, stop talking, get to work, or lower your voice. It is best to keep it to one or two words and be consistent with use.

NOTE: The focus of this collection of ideas has been prevention. Choose what works best for you and your students. When the prevention strategy is not working, you may see the student start to move through the behavior escalation cycle, so more intentional support may be necessary. This next section is to help you or the school behavior team analyze student behavior and find an appropriate intervention to offer behavior support.

Seven Phases of Behavior Escalation: How Do We Respond?

According to Dr. Reesha Adamson, an associate professor in the Department of Counseling, Leadership, and Special Education at Missouri State University, "recognizing and intervening in each of the seven phases of a crisis cycle can help meet teacher and student de-escalation needs and ideally prevent intense behaviors."[10]

The Seven Phases of Behavior Escalation developed by Dr. Geoff Colvin and Dr. George Sugai is widely accepted as the model for understanding and responding to the various stages a student goes through prior to, during, and after a behavior event. See the chart, which is based on their model.[11]

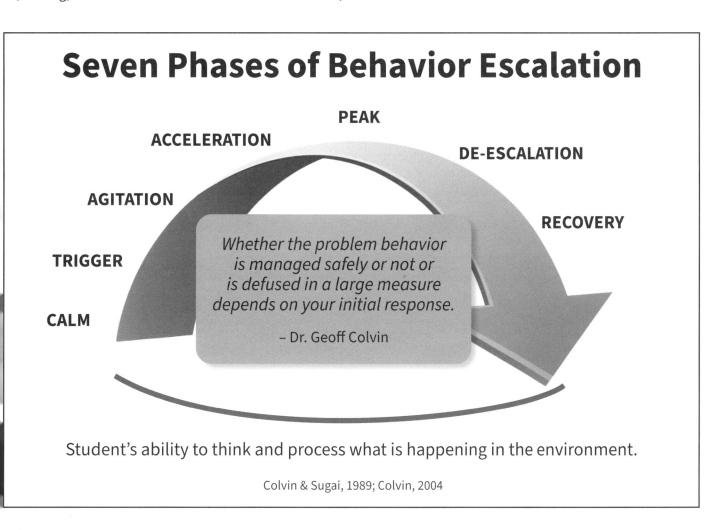

Seven Phases of Behavior Escalation

PEAK

ACCELERATION

DE-ESCALATION

AGITATION

RECOVERY

TRIGGER

Whether the problem behavior is managed safely or not or is defused in a large measure depends on your initial response.

– Dr. Geoff Colvin

CALM

Student's ability to think and process what is happening in the environment.

Colvin & Sugai, 1989; Colvin, 2004

The best time to intervene is as soon as the student is triggered or we observe signs of agitation. Of course, teachers don't always see these two stages, so acceleration is often the first time the adult is aware of the problem. The De-Escalation Strategies Chart and Student Escalation Planning Tool are resources to help teachers plan an effective response at each of the stages. There is not one "right" way, but the adult's response is the critical constant for any strategy to work.

The De-Escalation Strategies Chart is based on the Seven Phases of Behavior Escalation and provides a quick list for what to look for in student behavior at each stage and possible responses from the adult.

The Behavior Escalation Planning Form is intended for team use to plan a consistent adult response to target behaviors across settings. You may choose to use responses from the De-Escalation Strategies Chart or create your own. Give yourself permission to do what works.

DE-ESCALATION STRATEGIES	
Student Behavior	**Teacher Strategies**
Calm • Participating in classroom routines • Helping pass out materials or equipment • Willing to work with a partner • Using positive language • Meeting expected behaviors	**Calm** • Prompt/pre-correct for expected behaviors • Ask student to assist or help in some way • Pair with a strategic peer • High rates of positive feedback
Triggers • Conflict with peer or teacher • Family stress/crisis • Tired/sick/hungry • Work too difficult/change in routines • Feeling criticized or embarrassed	**Triggers-Focus on Prevention and Redirection** • Ask questions that are helpful – Is everything ok? Can I help? • Verbally remind: "Remember the two things you can do if you don't know/need help/feel frustrated, etc." • Redirect nonverbally or speak in private, if possible • Allow student to take a break/run errand
Agitation • Mumbling, frustrated comments • Heavy breathing, exasperation • Hands/legs start to tap or become fidgety • Eyes dart around the room • Excessive movement • Provokes peers	**Agitation-Focus on Reducing Anxiety** • Show empathy, communicate concern • Speak in calm, quiet voice • Redirect student to engage in a task • Offer time in a calming area/calming activity • Offer choices • Suggest they speak with preferred adult
Acceleration • Arguing • Refusing to follow directions • Complains about adult directions/assignments • Destroys materials/rips up paper	**Acceleration-Focus is on Safety** • Pause and assess – is this an emergency? • Avoid escalation – threats, loud voice • Provide choice to work independently at alternative workspace • Privately prompt the student to problem-solve outside the room
Peak • Hits/Kicks desk or furniture • Uses obscenities toward teacher/peers • Pushes materials off desk • Storms out of classroom • Physical altercation with peer	**Peak-Focus is on Implementing the Safety Plan** • Student and staff safety first • Teach the class how to clear the room • Inform all students what to do and assure safety • Crisis plan in place and activated, if any concern for danger
De-Escalation • Not ready to accept responsibility for actions • Focuses on who they perceive caused the problem • May want to act like it didn't happen • Eager for forgiveness	**De-Escalation-Focus is on Removing Attention** • Allow student space to calm down with supervision • Provide opportunity for nonjudgmental discussion • Determine if removing from class or staying to re-group • Planned ignoring strategy • Prompt self-management strategies and walk away
Recovery • Eager to move on/wants to avoid further discussion • Friendly/calm • Tries to reconnect with adult	**Recovery-Focus on Debrief/Problem Solving** • Help student get back into routine • Provide reflective or restorative opportunity • Return to task and offer choices • Remind the student that they can improve, and you will help • Move forward with planned consequence with empathy • Use problem-solving sheet to de-brief the situation and make a plan for next time; what to do before escalating

Student Behavior Escalation Planning Form

STUDENT RESPONSES

Calm Cooperative	Triggers Unresolved Conflicts	Agitation Unfocused	Acceleration Focused/Intense	Peak Most Severe	De-Escalation Confused	Recovery Non-engage/Alone

SPECIFIC STAFF OR ADULT RESPONSE

Prevention	Prevention and Redirection	Reduce Anxiety	Safety	Crisis Intervention	Remove Excess Attention	Re-Establish Routines

Adapted from Bounds (2003)
Lewis, Kittleman, & Wilcox (2011)

Teacher Directions:

Student Response

- The team should discuss and fill in each box based on observations.
- Calm: List the behaviors typically observed when the student is calm.
- Triggers: What are triggers of the target behavior? (ABC Data form in Section Three is an effective tool to figure this out.)
- Agitation: List specific behaviors observed when the student is agitated.
- Acceleration: List specific behaviors observed when student behavior accelerates.
- Continue to fill in specific behaviors observed for Peak, De-Escalation, and Recovery phases.
- Remove excess attention: Have a plan in place for 1:1 quiet support if possible or make alternate plans for minimal attention as the student tries to self-regulate.
- Re-establish routines: The goal is to have the student return to class and get back to work, normal schedule, and routines. This step can be difficult for multiple parties. If the other students and staff have been impacted by the event, some are not ready to move on even if the student is ready to do so. It is important to prepare and train staff and students on how to recover. Restorative Practices/Circles are a great tool for re-entry after an explosive event.

Specific Staff/Adult Response

- Prevention/Redirection: Plan adult responses such as behaviors that will be ignored, phrases to use in response to behavior, as well as plans to redirect.
- Reduce Anxiety: List calming strategies that have been taught to the student and that the student/ adults have agreed are appropriate and desirable.
- Safety: A safety plan should be developed and shared with all parties in the event the behavior becomes a danger to student(s) or staff. This may include removal of student, removal of specific furniture or materials, class evacuation using a code word, and other school or district-approved safety measures.
- Crisis Intervention: List the members of the team who are called at this phase to assist in de-escalation and implementation of safety plan protocols. List the responsibilities of each person. List phone numbers or any other means of communication for easy access.

BEHAVIOR PROBLEM-SOLVING

Behavior Problem-Solving Tools

Behavior Problem-Solving is the process in which educators take steps to look at problem behavior as an unmet need to resolve rather than a person to "fix." Initially, this may include informal problem-solving where only one teacher reflects on and analyzes a student's behavior and tries to make changes in their own room. Several forms and tools are included in this chapter to help organize this informal process.

Behavior Problem-Solving may also include a school-based team that meets to discuss and develop a plan for behaviors that occur across multiple locations. The team will solicit parent approval and input; conduct observations and interviews; collect and analyze data; and create a Behavior Intervention Plan. It is a requirement and best practice to include and collaborate with the student and caregivers throughout the process, especially if the process goes beyond the involvement of one teacher. Dr. Ross Greene's quote, "Kids do well if they can," are powerful words that guide the team to separate a student's behavior from who they are as a person and find ways to support them in their attempts at behavior improvement.

ABC Data Forms

An ABC Data Form is used as an observation tool to gather information that will be useful in developing a Behavior Intervention Plan (BIP) or to analyze and plan changes to the classroom environment. ABC refers to:

- **A**ntecedent (Trigger): the events, action, or circumstances that happen before the target behavior
- **B**ehavior: the target behavior
- **C**onsequences: the action or response that follows the behavior—does not have to be punitive; includes any action that follows the behavior

The ABC is usually considered a direct observation format because someone should be directly observing the behavior when it happens. Typically, it is a format that is used when an external observer is available who has the time and ability to observe and document behaviors during specified periods of the day.

Tear-Sheet Data Collection

An easy way to track the frequency of a behavior, or gather baseline data, is called "tear sheet" data.

✓ Use a large rectangular sticky note or fold a piece of copy paper in half.

✓ On the edge of each side, label or code what specific target behavior (Bx) you are counting (BL=blurt, OT = on task, NOT = not on task, etc.)

✓ Carry the paper around for at least an hour, three different times.

✓ Use a new piece of paper each time and record the date and start/end times.

✓ Each time the student exhibits the target Bx, make a tiny tear on the appropriate edge.

✓ At the end of the hour, count the tears.

✓ No technology, no pencil, and no public awareness needed.

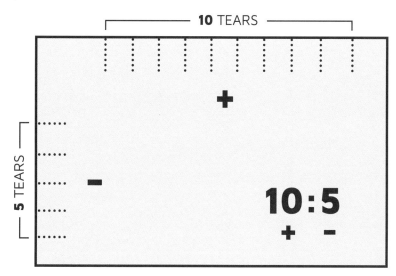

ABC Data Form

The ABC is usually considered a direct observation format because someone should be directly observing the behavior when it happens. Typically, it is a format that is used when an external observer is available who has the time and ability to observe and document behaviors during specified periods of the day.

Student: _____   Date: _____

Class/Teacher: _____   Observer: _____

Activity: _____   Other Information: _____

Time	Antecedent	Behavior	Consequences

ABC Hypothesis Form

Setting or Event	Antecedent (Trigger) *What Happens Before the Bx?*	Target Behavior *Describe Specifically.*	Consequence *Maintaining Behavior*
Example: In Math class	When a new assignment is given.	Taylor knocks her paper on the floor and screams, "I won't do it!" repeatedly.	Taylor is sent into the hallway and escapes work.

Five-Minute FBA

The goal of the Five-Minute FBA is to hypothesize how a specific behavior is serving a student. Anyone who has ever conducted a full Functional Behavioral Assessment (FBA) knows there is no such thing as getting it done in five minutes. This is the informal pre-work or reflection that anyone can employ before behavior escalates to requiring more time and support. When you have had some time apart from the student, reflect and try the following steps. You may choose to use the Five-Minute FBA Form.

1. Write a description of the target behavior you would like to help the student improve. Be sure behaviors are described in observable, measurable terms. Examples:

   a. Blurts out answers 15–20 times per hour vs. Disruptive

   b. Argues in a loud tone with adults when corrected vs. Disrespectful

   c. Puts hands on others with intent to harm vs. Aggressive

2. Collect data on frequency, time of day, etc., to identify patterns at two separate times. (Tear sheet data!)

3. Next to each target behavior, hypothesize what the child is getting or getting out of with that specific behavior.

4. Consider what skill deficit(s) are contributing to the behavior and how you or another adult can provide teaching and support.

5. Consider any environmental factors within your control that you can modify.

6. Teach a replacement behavior to the student.

7. Affirm the replacement behavior with planned attention every time you see it.

Get Me Out of Trouble Plan

Adapted from *Hanging In* by Jeffrey Benson

The plan has four parts:

- ✓ These things make me upset or mad quickly:

- ✓ Ways I can avoid the things that upset me:

- ✓ Steps I can take to keep calm when things are starting to upset me:

- ✓ My escape plan—where to go if nothing else works:

This is a brief list that can be written out with a student to plan for difficult times when self-regulation is a struggle. We want to coach kids to recognize 1) their triggers, 2) how to avoid them, 3) how to stay calm, and 4) who to see for assistance. Each part of the plan helps build the student's confidence in their own abilities to manage stressful situations rather than always waiting for an adult to do so. If working with younger students, it is recommended that each part of the plan has pictures in addition to words.

Five-Minute FBA FORM

Student Name: _____ Age:____ Grade:____ Date: _____

Person(s) completing the form: _____

Student Info: _____

_____

Student Strengths: _____

_____

1. Description of the Target Behavior:

What does the target behavior(s) look like?
How often does the target behavior(s) occur?
How long does the target behavior(s) last?
How disruptive or dangerous is the target behavior(s)?

2. Description of the Antecedent (Trigger)

When, where, and with whom are problem behaviors most likely?

Schedule (Times)	Activity	Specific Target Behavior	Likelihood of Problem Behavior	Frequency of Behavior
			Low High 1 2 3 4 5	
			1 2 3 4 5	
			1 2 3 4 5	
			1 2 3 4 5	
			1 2 3 4 5	

3. Purpose of Behavior:

Target Behavior	Gain	Escape

4. Are there any skill deficits contributing to the behavior (academic, emotional, etc.)?

_____

_____

5. Any environmental factors that can be modified/changed (schedule, location, timing, sound, etc.)?

_____

_____

6. Replacement Behaviors

New/Replacement Behavior (Describe what the student should do instead of the Target Behavior)	Who Will Teach It?	How Will It Be Reinforced?	Behavior a. Decreased b. Increased c. Stayed the Same

Get Me Out of Trouble Plan

Adapted from *Hanging In* by Jeffrey Benson

Name:_____

These things make me upset or mad quickly:

_____

_____

_____

Ways I can avoid the things that upset me:

_____

_____

_____

Steps I can take to keep calm when things are starting to upset me:

_____

_____

_____

My escape plan—where to go if nothing else works:

_____

_____

_____

Behavior Checklists

The next few pages are various behavior checklists/point sheets that can be used as behavior tracking tools. Choose the form that best fits your daily schedule, the behavior you are tracking, and the age of the student. Regardless of what type of tracking/checklist you use, I suggest the following:

Helpful Hints:

✓ Write the behavior to track in specific, positive language (Ex.: Raised a quiet hand and waited, stayed seated until given permission, used the Four-Word Strategy to make requests, used safe hands, used school-appropriate words).

✓ Use a scale vs. yes/no. Suggested scale: 3 = 0–1 prompts from adult, 2 = 2–3 prompts from adult, and 1 = more than 3 prompts. I do not use 0 because even if the student gets all 1s, they do not meet the goal—no need for extreme failure; failure by itself is enough.

✓ Use blue or black ink to complete the daily point sheet.

Included in the resources are these great Behavior Tracking Forms:

1. Target Behavior and Replacement Behavior Tracking Form

2. Doing Good Things Form

3. WOW Card

4. Weekly Behavior Chart

Behavior Agreement

A Behavior Agreement or Contract is a simple document with the behavior goals, privileges, consequences, and supports that the student and teacher agree upon. Putting all the agreements in writing creates understanding and trust while providing documentation for review if questions arise.

Target Behavior and Replacement Form

Name: _____   Date: ____ / ____ / ____

Target Behaviors	BREAKFAST	SPECIALS	MATH	ELA	READING	LUNCH	RECESS
State behavior positively.	3 2 1	3 2 1	3 2 1	3 2 1	3 2 1	3 2 1	3 2 1
	3 2 1	3 2 1	3 2 1	3 2 1	3 2 1	3 2 1	3 2 1

Points Possible _____ Points Received _____ % of Points _____ Goal Met _____

Replacement Behavior	BREAKFAST	SPECIALS	MATH	ELA	READING	LUNCH	RECESS
List replacement behaviors. Tally by location.							

I used my coping skills _____ times today!

3	Great day! I used kind words and hands, feet, and materials appropriately for the time period. I did not need to be redirected or prompted for appropriate behavior.
2	Good day! I used kind words and hands, feet, and materials appropriately most of the block. I had to be redirected or prompted one to three times.
1	Okay day. I struggled to use kind words and hands, feet and materials appropriately in this block. I had to be prompted or redirected more than three times.

GOAL _____   My Points today _____

I am working for (Circle **ONE**):   Puzzle Time   Tech Time   Free Play Time   Positive Phone Call Home

Doing Good Things Form

BLOCK	MON	TUES	WED	THURS	FRI
Objectives					
Refrains from talking with peers during instruction	3 2 1	3 2 1	3 2 1	3 2 1	3 2 1
Begins class within first 3 minutes	3 2 1	3 2 1	3 2 1	3 2 1	3 2 1
Brings book, notebook, pen, and agenda to class	3 2 1	3 2 1	3 2 1	3 2 1	3 2 1
Stay in your seat/One get up activity with permission	3 2 1	3 2 1	3 2 1	3 2 1	3 2 1

Comments:

BLOCK	MON	TUES	WED	THURS	FRI
Objectives					
Refrains from talking with peers during instruction	3 2 1	3 2 1	3 2 1	3 2 1	3 2 1
Begins class within first 3 minutes	3 2 1	3 2 1	3 2 1	3 2 1	3 2 1
Brings book, notebook, pen, and agenda to class	3 2 1	3 2 1	3 2 1	3 2 1	3 2 1
Stay in your seat/One get up activity with permission	3 2 1	3 2 1	3 2 1	3 2 1	3 2 1

Comments:

BLOCK	MON	TUES	WED	THURS	FRI
Objectives					
Refrains from talking with peers during instruction	3 2 1	3 2 1	3 2 1	3 2 1	3 2 1
Begins class within first 3 minutes	3 2 1	3 2 1	3 2 1	3 2 1	3 2 1
Brings book, notebook, pen, and agenda to class	3 2 1	3 2 1	3 2 1	3 2 1	3 2 1
Stay in your seat/One get up activity with permission	3 2 1	3 2 1	3 2 1	3 2 1	3 2 1

Comments:

BLOCK	MON	TUES	WED	THURS	FRI
Objectives					
Refrains from talking with peers during instruction	3 2 1	3 2 1	3 2 1	3 2 1	3 2 1
Begins class within first 3 minutes	3 2 1	3 2 1	3 2 1	3 2 1	3 2 1
Brings book, notebook, pen, and agenda to class	3 2 1	3 2 1	3 2 1	3 2 1	3 2 1
Stay in your seat/One get up activity with permission	3 2 1	3 2 1	3 2 1	3 2 1	3 2 1

Comments:

BLOCK	MON	TUES	WED	THURS	FRI
Objectives					
Refrains from talking with peers during instruction	3 2 1	3 2 1	3 2 1	3 2 1	3 2 1
Begins class within first 3 minutes	3 2 1	3 2 1	3 2 1	3 2 1	3 2 1
Brings book, notebook, pen, and agenda to class	3 2 1	3 2 1	3 2 1	3 2 1	3 2 1
Stay in your seat/One get up activity with permission	3 2 1	3 2 1	3 2 1	3 2 1	3 2 1

3 = 0-1 points			
2 = 2-3 points			
1 = more than 3 prompts			

WEEK OF:_____   **PARENT SIGNATURE:**_____

Goal: 85% (51 points for the week) = _____ **reward**   **80% (48 points for the week) =** _____

WOW CARD

Name: _____

My Goal(s): _____

Parent Signature: _____

Date: _____

86 points/90% = ___

77 points/80% = ___

1 = Not Met 2 = Ok/Tried 3 = Excellent	**Be Respectful** 1. 2.	**Be Responsible** 1. 2.	**Be Safe** 1. 2.	My Own Goal	Teacher Initials	WOW!!! Comments
1st	3 2 1	3 2 1	3 2 1	3 2 1		
2nd	3 2 1	3 2 1	3 2 1	3 2 1		
3rd	3 2 1	3 2 1	3 2 1	3 2 1		
4th	3 2 1	3 2 1	3 2 1	3 2 1		
5th	3 2 1	3 2 1	3 2 1	3 2 1		
6th	3 2 1	3 2 1	3 2 1	3 2 1		
7th	3 2 1	3 2 1	3 2 1	3 2 1		
8th	3 2 1	3 2 1	3 2 1	3 2 1		
TOTAL /96	/24	/24	/24	/24		

Privilege Earned: _____

_____ Behavior Chart   Date/Week of: _____

	MONDAY		TUESDAY		WEDNESDAY		THURSDAY		FRIDAY	
	Completes Work/ On Task	Does Not Argue With Adults	Completes Work/ On Task	Does Not Argue With Adults	Completes Work/ On Task	Does Not Argue With Adults	Completes Work/ On Task	Does Not Argue With Adults	Completes Work/ On Task	Does Not Argue With Adults
Reading Lesson	3 2 1	3 2 1	3 2 1	3 2 1	3 2 1	3 2 1	3 2 1	3 2 1	3 2 1	3 2 1
Reading Group/ Workstations	3 2 1	3 2 1	3 2 1	3 2 1	3 2 1	3 2 1	3 2 1	3 2 1	3 2 1	3 2 1
Language Arts/ Writing	3 2 1	3 2 1	3 2 1	3 2 1	3 2 1	3 2 1	3 2 1	3 2 1	3 2 1	3 2 1
Lunch	3 2 1	3 2 1	3 2 1	3 2 1	3 2 1	3 2 1	3 2 1	3 2 1	3 2 1	3 2 1
Math Lesson	3 2 1	3 2 1	3 2 1	3 2 1	3 2 1	3 2 1	3 2 1	3 2 1	3 2 1	3 2 1
Recess	3 2 1	3 2 1	3 2 1	3 2 1	3 2 1	3 2 1	3 2 1	3 2 1	3 2 1	3 2 1
Math Group/ Workstation	3 2 1	3 2 1	3 2 1	3 2 1	3 2 1	3 2 1	3 2 1	3 2 1	3 2 1	3 2 1
Science/ Social Studies	3 2 1	3 2 1	3 2 1	3 2 1	3 2 1	3 2 1	3 2 1	3 2 1	3 2 1	3 2 1
Dismissal	3 2 1	3 2 1	3 2 1	3 2 1	3 2 1	3 2 1	3 2 1	3 2 1	3 2 1	3 2 1
Fill in your own.	3 2 1	3 2 1	3 2 1	3 2 1	3 2 1	3 2 1	3 2 1	3 2 1	3 2 1	3 2 1
TOTAL POINTS	/60		/60		/60		/60		/60	

Points Earned

50-60 = GREAT DAY
(reward of choice)

****

44-49 = GOOD DAY
(sticker earned)

Privileges

Coupon Caddy
Homework Pass
Tech Time
Positive Call Home
Class Bonus Choice
Positive Note Home

Weekly Points (240 Goal)

Monday _____
Tuesday _____
Wednesday _____
Thursday _____
Friday _____
_____/300 = _____%

ANECDOTAL NOTES:

Monday: _____

Tuesday: _____

Wednesday: _____

Thursday: _____

Friday: _____

Student Name:_____ Date: _____

Behavior Agreement

To help _____ improve classroom behavior and overall academic performance we have developed this contract.

I will commit to meeting the following behavior goals:

1. _____

2. _____

3. _____

If I am successful, I will earn:

_____

_____

_____

If I do not show the behaviors listed above, my consequences are:

_____

_____

_____

The teacher commits to the following supports:

_____

_____

_____

Student Signature: _____

Teacher Signature: _____

Parent Signature: _____

Sample Letter to Parent

If a student needs additional support for behavior, the parent/caregiver should be notified and included in the decision-making process. We want the parent/caregiver to know we feel they have an important role in their student's success, so our language and timing is extremely important.

Dear parent/guardian,

We believe that you have a very important role in the success of your student's school year, and we appreciate your expertise when it comes to knowing your student and what is best for them.

We are excited about a support program called _____. This program helps students improve their behavior by giving them feedback throughout the day on their choices. Your student will be assigned a mentor (another staff member at our school). Each morning, students "check in" with their mentor, review their behavior expectations, and set a goal of how many points they will earn that day to earn a bonus privilege.

As your student goes through each class, they will receive feedback and earn points for positive behavior on the point sheet. At the end of the day your student will "check out" with their mentor (staff member) who will total the points and discuss how the day went. If your student earns the goal for that day, they also earn a privilege. Most privileges are provided in the mentor teacher's classroom, such as computer time, a sticker, homework pass, etc.

_____ has been chosen to participate in this support system. We are excited that you will be a part of our plan to help them be respectful, responsible, and safe at school. We want to partner with you in this program, so we ask that you please sign your student's daily point sheet every day and return it back to school. We are hopeful that you will have a conversation with them about how the day went and provide them with encouragement for improvement. If you have any questions, please contact me at 555-555-5555 or name@email.org.

Sincerely,

BEHAVIOR SUPPORT TOOLS

This section provides several options for simple tools that will help the student meet their targeted behavior goals. A formula for success for any tool is that it's appealing to the student and manageable for the adult. Each of these individual strategies incorporates brief intervals of time in which the student is attempting to meet a specific goal. Each time the goal is met, the student receives positive feedback and tracking of progress. Once the pre-determined number of intervals have been achieved, the goal is met, and a privilege is earned.

Helpful Hints:

✓ Use the strategy for a minimum of 10 days before determining effectiveness.

✓ Focus on positive progress and use positive language/"I" statements.

✓ Use nonverbal reminders when possible (Correction Cards, Code Word).

✓ When reminders or corrections must be made, use a quiet business-like voice.

✓ Use the same brief statement each time ("Safe hands, Level One voice").

✓ **Avoid threatening language** or constantly reminding student of what they will lose/punitive consequences.

Picture Points (Elementary)

Allow the student to choose one of the following pictures to use as a tracking tool of progress toward a goal.

Teacher Directions:

- Establish the behavioral goal. "Jenna will use safe hands for 20 minutes."
- Decide the time interval (5, 10, 15, 20, or 30-minute intervals)
- Each time the student meets the goal during the time interval they connect one set of picture points.
- When the picture points are all traced, the student can color in the picture and choose a privilege for the entire class.
  - Ideas include three-minute dance video, five-minute talk or tech time, extra recess, make and watch a two-minute class video, favorite class game at the end of the day, etc.

Sticky Note Flag Strategy

This strategy is to help keep track of reminders given to the student.

Teacher Directions:

- Place a row of five sticky note flags on the student's desk or in a place they can see them. (You can choose a different number, but I recommend at least three.)
- Number them 1, 2, 3, 4, 5. You may write a positive note or bonus opportunity on 3, 4, and 5 or just 4 and 5 to motivate the student to keep those final reminders (Class point, two Dojo points, Positive Note Home, etc).
- When the student displays target behavior, remove one flag and stay silent or encourage positively.
- If student loses all flags, they do not earn privileges and caregiver may be notified if that is part of the plan.
- You can allow them to earn a flag back for excellent efforts.

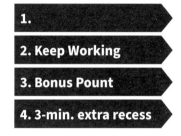

Correction Cards
(See Chapter 3 for this nonverbal tool for reminders)

Connection Cards

These small cards with words of affirmation are used to nonverbally recognize students who are meeting behavioral and character goals. Students who struggle with behavior tend to dictate teacher attention, so this tool allows other students to receive adult attention as well.

Teacher Directions:

- Print, laminate, and cut out cards.
- Place on student's desk when student is meeting or exceeding expectations.
- Student can return the card to a central location or keep if not laminated.

Picture Points

Name:_____   Goal:_____ Date:_____

Each picture point connection = _____ minutes.

I am working to earn _____.

Picture Points

Name:_____   Goal:_____   Date: _____

Each picture point connection = _____ minutes.

I am working to earn _____.

Picture Points

Name:_____   Goal:_____   Date: _____

Each picture point connection = _____ minutes.

I am working to earn _____.

Connection Cards

You CAN do it!

I BELIEVE in YOU.

YOU ARE DOING AWESOME!

Yay!

GREAT JOB!

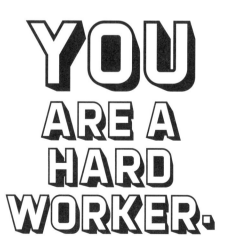

YOU ARE A HARD WORKER.

Character Cubes (Unifix cubes)

This strategy has been very successful for students I have taught or supported.

Teacher Directions:

- Use the math cubes that are found in every elementary school!
- Write needed letters on the blocks to spell a word that is meaningful to the student. Examples: Success, Bonus Time, Amazing, Class Hero, etc.
- Set the predetermined goal and time interval for a target behavior.
- Each time the goal is met, the student connects a letter. When the word is spelled the privilege is earned.

Blurt Tally

Alternately, you could spell the word BLURT on cubes and remove a cube for each verbal disruption. The student receives a point for each letter kept and 10 points = earned privilege.

> **NOTE:** Chapter 7 includes many tools from which to choose to assist in behavior problem solving and behavior support in your classroom. Please choose one or two ideas that help solve an issue you are currently facing.

De-Escalation, Behavior Support, and Behavior Problem-Solving
Chapter 7 Roadmap (Planning Guide)

Activity Choose 1 from each section	**Action Items:** What do you need to complete?	**Date:** When do you plan to use?	**Page #**
DE-ESCALATION/LANGUAGE OF DISAGREEMENT			
Four-Word Strategy			
Affective or "I" Statements			
Decision-Makers Basket			
Breathing Exercises			
Calming Apps			
Code Word			
Behavior Escalation Planning Form			
BEHAVIOR PROBLEM-SOLVING			
ABC Data Form			
Tear-Sheet Data Collection			
Five-Minute FBA			
Get Me Out of Trouble Plan			
Behavior Checklists			
Behavior Agreement			
BEHAVIOR SUPPORT TOOLS			
Picture Points (Elementary)			
Sticky Note Flag Strategy			
Correction Cards			
Connection Cards			
Character Cubes			
Blurt Tally			

CHAPTER EIGHT

Teacher-Family Relationship Tips

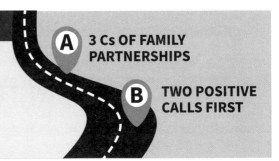

A 3 Cs OF FAMILY PARTNERSHIPS

B TWO POSITIVE CALLS FIRST

Coming together is a beginning; keeping together is progress; working together is success. – Henry Ford

A positive, collaborative relationship between parents and teachers has been shown to improve students' academic achievement, social relationships, and emotional well-being. When we work together with parents, students do better in school and at home, and it makes our year feel more successful professionally.

This book has cited the 3 Cs—Connected, Capable, and Calm—for students throughout the chapters as basic needs that students of all ages are seeking to have met. The parent/teacher relationship calls for its own set of the 3 Cs: Communication, Collaboration, and Compassion.

In order to build trust, we start with Communication. Creating a system of communication that works for you and your students' families is crucial to the success of your partnerships. Whether you decide to do something weekly, bi-weekly, or through a monthly email/newsletter/blog post (see the downloadable resources for a sample template), the method should be consistent. Parents come to trust and depend on the information to arrive as we promise, so we want to deliver as consistently as possible. The amount of communication with families is heavy in the beginning with collection of both required and optional forms but should be quickly streamlined into intermittent and consistent communication that is helpful, organized, and brief.

A   3 Cs OF FAMILY PARTNERSHIPS

Tips for Successful Communication

- **Choose one or two methods.** Too many places to post and check becomes overwhelming for everyone.
- **Keep it brief.** Less than two minutes to read is ideal.
- **Use a consistent visual format** so parents can quickly view the areas that apply to them.
- **Keep it positive.** Share good news and general news. If something specific is not going well, communicate with certain families or send a separate email from your weekly communication.
- **Highlight a student/students** each time for doing something well. Be sure all students make the list sometime throughout the year—even if it's on a list of twenty names! I love the VIP—Very Improved Person—because everyone will improve in some way over the year.

Everyone agrees that when parents and teachers collaborate as allies and teammates, it has a positive impact on student performance and their emotional well-being. We create a safety net of caring adults who are focused on the best interests of children. Many of us have experienced a parent-teacher relationship that became negative or adversarial, and simply put, it is stressful and draining. When we collaborate with parents, which includes some give and take, we create opportunities for honest dialogue where both parties feel comfortable reaching out when challenges arise. When we feel and receive family support, it makes our year and our job feel like the success we worked so hard to achieve.

Tips for Successful Collaboration

- **Communicate positively first.** Begin open conversations with what is going well.
- **Refer to the parent/caregiver as the "expert" on their student.** They are the most knowledgeable.
- **Refer to your relationship as a team.** Allow equal voice from family members.
- **Be open and listen to their ideas.** Write down what you hear, paraphrase, and repeat back to them so they know you are actively listening.
- If you are unable to fulfill a request, **be prepared to share a resource** (other staff member, book, website, agency) that might help them.

Compassion is a key component in the parent/teacher relationship as there are few things more fulfilling or more uncertain than raising or teaching a child. It's an unpredictable experience that unfortunately doesn't come with a set of instructions. (I've searched!) It is important to consider that we each have different perspectives when approaching a student's educational needs, but we share the same end goal: student success. When parents send their children to school, they are sharing this cherished experience with teachers, people who have studied to be experts in working with children, oftentimes having never met them. This creates a vulnerability for parents who may feel judged about their parenting practices or who don't perceive the positive intent behind some teacher practices. These two feelings alone can cause divisive and defensive thoughts and language to slowly creep into communication. When we recognize and accept their vulnerability and our own, we can act with compassion even when communication becomes difficult. Strong parent-teacher relationships are built on compassion, and respectful communication. Collaboration with parents allows us to connect with our students and help them reach their full potential.

Tips for Compassionate Communication

- **Try to consider the perspective of the parent.** This is their "baby" regardless of their age or issue. Respect that bond.
- **Use "I feel" statements** when communicating something difficult (rather than "Your child…").
- **Show willingness to listen and help**—with boundaries.
- **Hear their suggestions.** Teachers usually know what's best for their class, but the parent is trying to share what they feel is best for their individual child. Hear them out—it may be surprisingly helpful.
- **Compassion is the counter for anger.** Our language matters: "I care for your child, and I care about your family. I will not give up." (rather than: "I don't know what else I can do.")
- **If you mess up, it's okay to apologize.** (I have multiple times.) It shows the parent that we make mistakes too.

Student Information Forms

✓ Family Information Form

✓ 5 Things to Know About

✓ Social Media Release Form

Family Information Form

Parent/Caregiver Name:_____

Student Name: _____

Relationship to Student: _____

What is the best way to contact you regarding your student?

☐ Email (Address: _____)

☐ Phone Call (Number:_____ Best Time to Call: _____)

☐ Other:_____

When would you like to be contacted?

☐ If my student does something amazing!

☐ If my student's grade drops below _____%.

☐ If my student receives a consequence for behavior.

☐ If my student is not participating in class activities.

☐ Other:_____

Is there anything else I need to know about your student? Please feel free to complete the Five Things to Know About or email at _____ .

Five Things to Know About

———————————————————————————————
(Student name)

Dear Parents/Caregivers:

I am so excited to have your student in my class this year. I value your expertise when it comes to knowing your student because you know them better than anyone else. Please share up to five things you feel I should know about your student to be the best teacher I can for them. This information is helpful in getting to know each of my students individually. Thank you!

1. _____
_____
_____

2. _____
_____
_____

3. _____
_____
_____

4. _____
_____
_____

5. _____
_____
_____

Social Media Release Form

Dear Parents/Caregivers:

I have created a class page on Twitter and Instagram. The purpose of these pages is to stay connected to families and explore learning on a new level through technology and social media. Our class Twitter and Instagram pages provide a fun, new way to share what is going on in our classroom as well as update you on important information. Please fill out the bottom portion of this form to grant permission to post photos and/ or videos of your student along with their work for school-related and educational purposes.

If you have any questions, please let me know. Thank you so much for your support and I look forward to connecting with you! You can follow our school online:

Twitter: @ _____

Instagram: @_____

Your name

_____

Please fill out and sign this consent form.

☐ I am the legal guardian of _____ and I give permission for my student to be photographed/recorded during school-related activities. I understand and agree to give _____ permission to post photos/videos of my student on our class social media pages (Twitter/Instagram) for educational purposes.

☐ I am the legal guardian of _____ and I **do not** give permission for my student to be included on social media sites. I do give permission for photographs to be taken to be shared with me or within the classroom only.

_____   _____
Parent/Caregiver Signature   Date

*Additional Notes: _____

_____

TWO POSITIVE CALLS FIRST

Some of the best advice I have ever been given was to contact a parent with good news before you ever have to contact with the opposite. The person who gave me this advice was a parent of one of my students! Let's just say that it wasn't what you might call "friendly" advice when I received it, but it was great advice nonetheless.

Most educators would agree that we know who the challenging students are within days of meeting them—sometimes minutes. This is when the planning of phone call #1 begins. As soon as the need for a parent call arises, begin thinking about the positive qualities you notice in the student, and make a quick call. Here is a sample of what this might sound like:

Positive Phone Call #1

Teacher: Hi, may I speak with the parent or guardian of _____, this is _____, from _____ (your school).

Hello, and thank you for taking my call. I am calling families this week to welcome each of you and your student to my class this year. I have already noticed how _____ _____ is (energetic, self-aware, good at making friends, verbally gifted, determined) and I can tell _____ is going to bring the energy! I would love to hear from you about _____'s past experiences in school so I can get a better understanding of what their needs are.

(Listen and take notes.)

Thank you so much for sharing this with me. Let me repeat what I heard you say: _____. Did I get that right? That is very helpful to me, and I appreciate your time and expertise when it comes to your student. Nobody knows more than you do. May I call on you in the future to ask for your help or share good news about _____? Be sure to call or email me anytime I can help you or _____. Have a great day/evening.

Follow up a few days later with Positive Phone Call #2.

Teacher: Hello _____,

I know you are busy, so thank you for taking my call. I had a few minutes to get a quick call in, so I am calling to let you know that I have noticed _____ trying to _____ this past week and I just wanted to share some good news. I am proud of their efforts, and I let them know in class today too.

As always, I appreciate your support, and reach out to me any time. Thank you.

If the parent is surprised or wants to ask about negative behaviors, I say this:

I have seen a few challenges with _____ this week, but we are working through that in class, and I will call you if it is something I need your help with. Thanks for checking.

Tips for Successful Phone Calls

Although calling a parent may take more preparation and time, there is no communication tool as powerful for building relationships, sharing enthusiasm, or conveying care. In the age of technology and so many options for electronic communication, the phone call is an often-avoided method due to the amount of extra time and effort it takes, but it helps to avoid miscommunication that often happens when parties misinterpret tone or intent over email or text.

- ✓ Prepare. Know your agenda/reason for calling and stick with it.
- ✓ Be ready to share some "little things" that you have taken the time to know.
- ✓ Have information you want to share in front of you so you don't have to fumble around looking for it, including grades and the school calendar.
- ✓ Highlight strengths. This will carry you through.
- ✓ Acknowledge the parent's expertise when it comes to their student.

Tips for Successful Face-to-Face Team Meetings

I have attended hundreds of parent meetings as a special education teacher meeting for IEPs and later as the RTI coordinator for our middle school. I have witnessed a lot of interesting adult behavior! There are a few things I have learned that truly seemed to help what could have been very difficult and volatile meetings stay on course. First, assume good will. Every parent, grandparent, or guardian who shows up, or doesn't show up to a meeting, loves their student. They are passionate and protective, and sometimes these two things might not translate positively in a stressful situation. Their methods of showing love may not align with your belief system, but assuming good will helps you focus on the student and what is needed to support them. Second, welcome the parent or caregiver. Welcome them as you would someone into your own home. I have heard that word used repeatedly by parents who came in upset and left happy: "Thank you for making us feel welcome."

- ✓ When the family arrives, have everyone in the meeting stand and ask the family members to sit first as "our guest." Then everyone else takes a seat around them.
- ✓ Open the meeting by introducing yourself and the parents and have any other members introduce themselves and share their role.
- ✓ Introduce the parents as "the Experts on Casey." This gives them a title as an expert in a room full of experts.
- ✓ State the reason for the meeting: We are all here today because we care about Casey, and we want to see her reach her full potential this year.
- ✓ Use a large piece of bulletin board or chart paper for the next step.
- ✓ Ask each member to share one or two qualities they admire about Casey and write them on the poster. Be sure to give all staff a heads up *before the meeting* that you will ask this question in the meeting. (I always asked the family if they wanted to keep the poster at the end of the meeting—100 percent took them home.)
- ✓ Take notes and read the notes out loud.
- ✓ Ask the family if they have questions throughout the meeting.
- ✓ Model "I feel" statements to help staff avoid labeling the student ("I feel disrespected when Casey uses swear words in my class" versus "Casey is disrespectful.")

- ✓ Thank everyone for their input and remind the family of all of the support the team is going to give their student. Thank them specifically for coming in to support the team.
- ✓ Set a date for when they can expect to hear from you.

It is recommended that teachers have at least one other staff member present if meeting with a parent who is upset or who has communicated that there is a problem. If that is not a possibility, check with your administrator to ask about the policy for recording a meeting with all parties' permission. Zoom, Google Meets, Teams, or a cell phone all offer this option so everyone is on the same page concerning what was discussed and agreed upon.

Final Thoughts

Creating a positive classroom community has become as critical to student learning and success as the content and the instructional techniques used to deliver that content. The world we live in is filled with an excess of tools to make our lives easier, more efficient, and more connected (social media, personal devices, etc.) but many of those same tools have made teaching and engaging students exponentially more difficult. Stepping back and remembering the basics of what humans need to be successful – feeling Connected, Capable, and Calm - can help us to focus on what matters most in our classrooms; helping our students find personal success while also learning how to be a contributing citizen in the world around them. I hope you use this roadmap to help you build your positive, supportive classroom community by finding ways to celebrate and respond to your students every day. Choose the ideas that help you to organize the methods, routines, and strategies that work for your setting. There is no one formula that fits every classroom. I encourage you to choose what feels manageable for you and go all in.

Finally, as you prepare for your year, your week, or your day working with students who need you now more than ever, please remember your final destination – your big goals for the students you teach. You chose this path because your heart told you that you have something to share that will help children. You were right, so share your gifts and share them well. You will be an important part of their journey, and what you do every day has a lasting impact on their lives!

Teach hard. Love harder.

Teacher-Family Relationship Tips
Chapter 8 Roadmap (Planning Guide)

Activity Choose 1 from each section	Action Items: What do you need to complete?	Date: When do you plan to use?	Page #
3 Cs OF FAMILY PARTNERSHIPS/STUDENTS FORMS			
Family Information Sheet			
Five Things to Know About			
Social Media Release Form			
TWO POSITIVE CALLS FIRST			
Positive Phone Call #1			
Positive Phone Call #2			

**DOWNLOADABLE RESOURCES
AND TEMPLATES**

The resources in this book are available for you
as a digital download!

Please visit **15minutefocusseries.com** and click this book cover
on the page. You will be directed to where you can access the
DOWNLOADABLE RESOURCES by entering this code:

BIWorkbook489